T0059708

TRANSFORM YOUR THINKING, TRANSFORM YOUR LIFE

*Radically Change Your Thoughts,
Your World, and Your Destiny*

DR. BILL WINSTON

Harrison House
Tulsa, Oklahoma

Unless otherwise indicated, all Scripture quotations are taken from the *King James Version* of the Bible.

Scripture quotations marked AMP are taken from the *Amplified® Bible.* Copyright © 1954, 1958, 1962, 1964, 1965, 1987 by The Lockman Foundation. Used by permission. (www.Lockman.org)

Scripture quotations marked (NIV) are taken from *The Holy Bible: New International Version®.* NIV®. Copyright © 1973, 1978, 1984 by International Bibl Society. Used by permission of Zondervan Publishing House. All rights reserved.

Scripture quotations marked (NASB) are taken from the *New American Standard Bible®,* Copyright © 1960,1962,1963,1968,1971,1972,1973,1975, 1977,1995 by The Lockman Foundation. Used by permission.

27 26 25 24 23   21 20 19 18 17

Transform Your Thinking, Transform Your Life:
Radically Change Your Thoughts, Your World, and Your Destiny
ISBN 13: 978-1-57794-971-8
ISBN 10: 1-57794-971-4
Copyright © 2008 by Dr. Bill Winston
P.O. Box 947
Oak Park, IL 60303

Published by Harrison House, Inc.
P.O. Box 35035
Tulsa, Oklahoma 74153
www.harrisonhouse.com

Printed in the United States of America. All rights reserved under International Copyright Law. Contents and/or cover may not be reproduced in whole or in part in any form without the express written consent of the Publisher.

TABLE OF CONTENTS

INTRODUCTION

The world is always telling us that we should be living the high life. Their idea of the high life is having a beer in our hand, sitting in a tropical paradise, and being surrounded by beautiful, wealthy people. Commercials and billboards picture "the high life" as idyllic landscapes and luxurious lifestyles. But what really is the high life?

Deep down inside, every human being knows what the high life is. The high life is being both happy and success-ful inside and out. It is something we all long for, but most of us believe it is impossible to achieve. The question is, why would God put that desire in us and then give us no way to realize it? He wouldn't! The Bible tells us that we can live the high life through Jesus Christ.

Jesus is the way to the high life, so why isn't every Christian living it? The Bible tells us why. **It says that we must first change the way we think.** Proverbs 23:7 says that we are what we think. That would mean that if we are poor, miserable, lonely, scared, sick, or frustrated and in a rage all the time—it is because of what we are thinking.

I heard it said once that we will always move in the direction of our most dominant thoughts. That is a profound truth! If we see ourselves working hard but never getting ahead, then we will probably continue to work hard and never get anywhere. We can be born again and filled with God's Spirit, but if we are constantly thinking of ourselves in terms of poverty and unhappiness, that is what we are going to experience in life.

There is good reason the Holy Spirit used the apostle Paul to literally beg Christians to attend to their minds.

> I beseech you therefore, brethren, by the mercies of God, that ye present your bodies a living sacrifice, holy, acceptable unto God, which is your reasonable service.
>
> And be not conformed to this world: but be ye transformed by the renewing of your mind, that ye may prove what is that good, and acceptable, and perfect, will of God.
>
> Romans 12:1-2

This says that when our minds are consumed with the Word of God, we will be transformed and move in the right direction. We will "prove" to the world around us what is the will of God, and His will is always truly good, fully acceptable, and perfect. The Bible makes it clear that God's will is for us to succeed and live in joy unspeakable and full of glory!

All this sounds simple enough. Just renew our minds or change the way we think by reading and studying the Word of God. Then all of us blood-bought, Spirit-filled believers should do just fine. However, I have noticed that many of us are not doing just fine. An example was during the last presidential election. I was amazed at the strife and contention *among the saints.* It became racial. It became mean. And it was a foul mess for the world to see. We certainly weren't proving the good, acceptable, and perfect will of God!

When the issues of politics or race or doctrine come up in your local church, when there is a family dispute over whose responsibility it is to feed the dog and take out the trash, when your boss calls you in to tell you that you are being laid off, or when your doctor tells you that you have a terrible disease, that is when you discover just how renewed your mind is! Do you act like the world or do you act like Jesus?

Personally, I have never been more built up and charged up since I began this study of how to renew my mind. I have discovered the vital importance of keeping it renewed. Understanding and going through this process has removed so many barriers and limitations I had placed on God's ability to move in my life—ways of seeing myself, my family, my church, and my God that had kept me from receiving everything Jesus died to give me. When I got serious about renewing my mind, I discovered the key to living the high life! For that reason alone I believe this is one of the most important books I have written.

As you read and meditate the Word of God presented here, as you take His Word to heart and allow it to change your perception of God, yourself, your life, and the world around you, you will be miraculously transformed. I can say this with full confidence not only because it is happening to me, but more important, because it is what God promised.

Jesus died to give you abundant life, the high life. The only thing that stands between you and living the high life is what is going on between your ears! Make the commitment to renew your mind, and let the revolutionary transformation of your life begin right now.

CHAPTER I

WHO'S GOT YOUR SOUL?

I beseech you therefore, brethren, by the mercies of God, that ye present your bodies a living sacrifice, holy, acceptable unto God, which is your reasonable service.

And be not conformed to this world: but be ye transformed by the renewing of your mind, that ye may prove what is that good, and acceptable, and perfect, will of God.

Romans 12:1-2

Christians are not to be conformed to this world. My paraphrased definition of the word *conformed* is to fashion and configure ourselves like this world, to adopt the customs of this world, and to be squeezed into the world's mold. From the moment we are conceived, the world and the spiritual enemies of God are bombarding us with thoughts that run contrary to the Word of God. They are in the business of keeping us from Jesus Christ so that they can control us.

If the world and the devil do not succeed in keeping us from Jesus Christ and we get saved, the real battle begins! We are not to continue to be conformed to this world; we are to be conformed to the image of Jesus. How does that happen? We are to be transformed by the renewing of our minds with God's Word. We have to change the way we think about everything.

The word *transformed* is translated from the Greek word *metamorphoo* {met-am-or-fo'-o},[1] which is where we get the English word metamorphosis. In elementary school we learned about metamorphosis by watching how a caterpillar spins its cocoon and later breaks out of the cocoon as a butterfly. The caterpillar completely changes its shape, coloring, and function. It goes from a worm-like creature that crawls on the ground to a bright-colored creature that flies gracefully through the air.

How are we to be transformed? What is our process of *metamorphoo?* Romans 12:2 says that it is the renewing of our minds. The word *renew* could also be translated *renovate.*[2] When we renovate a house, we tear out and throw away all the old, unwanted walls and decorations and replace them with brand-new ones. Sometimes we put in new furniture and appliances we have never used before. That is the picture the Holy Spirit gives us when He tells us that we are to be transformed by the renewing of our minds. He moves in and begins to renovate our soul with the Word of God. He tears down strongholds of deception and lies and replaces them with the truth. And one of the first things He begins to show us is who we are.

WHO ARE YOU?

It's a sad thing when people live their whole lives and never understand what it means to be a human being. They spend all their years trying to find out who they are and why they were created, but they never go to their Creator. If they did a little reading in the Bible, they would see that God created us in three parts: spirit, soul, and body.

> The very God of peace sanctify you wholly; and I pray God your whole spirit and soul and body be preserved blameless unto the coming of our Lord Jesus Christ.
>
> 1 Thessalonians 5:23

Our spirit, soul, and body are intimately connected and work together. Our spirit is the part of us that communicates with God. We were created to walk in communion with Him at all times. Under this spiritual headship is our soul, which is our mind, emotions, and will. Then our soul, in agreement with our spirit and God's Spirit, tells our physical body what to feel, say, and do. Although our physical body is our contact with the natural, physical world, it is not supposed to be in charge. Our spirits are to be in charge.

Our spirit life is superior to the physical, natural, and material life. The spirit is the highest form of living because our spirit man communicates with the Holy Spirit, who connects us back to God, our Source. The senses constitute a lower level of living so we must not allow our five senses to dominate. Therefore, we must renew our mind to the Word of God or it will be carnal.

We were originally created to live from our spirits in full submission to our Lord. God placed in human beings the desire to love and to be loved by Him. Our souls, which contain our thought, emotion, and will, are supposed to operate according to our communication with God. We were never meant to operate on the basis of our contact with the natural, physical world.

The fall of mankind occurred because Adam and Eve acted upon communication from the outside world, from the serpent, instead of communication with God on the inside, in their spirits. When we act according to our senses and our natural thinking, we can be easily deceived and sin against God. That's what happened to Adam and Eve.

WHAT WENT WRONG?

In the Garden of Eden Adam and Eve were living the high life. They had every material thing they needed or wanted. They were healthy and happy. They loved and honored each other and accomplished great things together. Their life was ideal. Their environment was perfect. And it was all based upon their intimate relationship with God.

One day God told Adam, "Don't eat of the tree of the knowledge of good and evil or you will die" in Genesis 2:17, and disaster ensued. Adam exercised the free will God had given him and ate of that tree. He acted on the counsel of the serpent instead of God's Word and made the wrong decision. He chose to disobey God, ate of the forbidden tree, and everything God had warned him about the tree came to pass. He immediately died.

Obviously, Adam and Eve didn't immediately die physically. They died spiritually. Death is permanent separation from a state of being, whether spiritual or natural. Initially, they died spiritually, which meant permanent separation from God. The Spirit of God and the eternal life of God left their human spirits.

Because Adam and Eve no longer lived in the state of eternal life, their souls and bodies began to decay. Without God's spiritual life in them, eventually they would die physically. Furthermore, they now lived primarily by what their physical senses and their natural minds told them. They had sunk to a very low level of living.

Human beings lost the high life when they lost their intimate relationship with God.

The result of Adam's sin not only affected him but the whole human race. As Adam's descendants, we were all born spiritually dead to God, cut off from Him for eternity. From the moment we were born we had to fight physical sickness and death. Satan was our spiritual lord and our minds were caught up in the material world instead of the spiritual Kingdom of God. Thank God, that was not the end of the story!

God sent Jesus to pay the price for Adam's sin and give us the opportunity to restore our spiritual life connection with Him. When we accept Jesus as our personal Lord and Savior, surrendering our lives to Him, we are born again spiritually. Our dead spirits are made alive by the Holy Spirit, who comes to live in us. We can communicate and fellowship freely with our Heavenly Father again. He returns us to the high life!

YOUR DIVINE CONNECTION

When you are born again your spirit is brand new, and it comes in line with the supernatural. The Holy Spirit lives in your new spirit. But your soul and body are another matter. Although they will be dramatically affected by the rebirth of your spirit, they are not brand new. They have not been regenerated yet. If you had dentures before you were saved, you probably will have dentures after you are saved unless God does a miracle. If you had a bad temper before you got saved, you will probably have to deal with your temper after you are saved. The difference is that now you are spiritually connected to God and your nature has changed. You are no longer under the influence of the devil. You are a child of God!

Believers are instantly restored to all the blessings of knowing God intimately, but the full manifestation of our new state of being is a process of maturity.

As a believer you still have battles with the devil, the world, and your flesh—only now you have God's ability to overcome and win the victory! Your divine connection is the difference between living the low life and living the high life.

Take wisdom and knowledge, for example. In the Garden of Eden before the Fall, there was no Northwestern, Harvard, or University of Southern California. There was no Museum of Natural History or Museum of Science and Industry. Adam and Eve received knowledge directly from the Source of all knowledge. The Holy Spirit lived inside them. They walked and talked with Jesus. And they communed with their Heavenly Father.

Educational institutions came after Adam sinned. Fallen human beings, separated from God, then received information from sources outside them instead of the Spirit and Word of God inside them. They went from the high life (living and learning from communication with God in their spirits) to the low life (living from their physical senses and natural thinking). The Word of God became a mystery to them, a dead letter to their souls, shrouded with mystery.

After our spirits are made alive and reconnected to our Heavenly Father at the new birth, God becomes our Instructor again. The Word of God becomes living and active in our lives. The Holy Ghost talks directly to our spirit, and we can get information and wisdom from Him by our spirit. We can still go to school and gain information, but we now understand that we process all that we learn by the Word and the Spirit of God.

> The spirit of a man is the candle of the Lord, searching all the inward parts of the belly.
>
> Proverbs 20:27

What is the purpose of a candle? It gives light, of course. Your spirit is the lighthouse of the Lord, where you receive revelation knowledge and understanding. His light shines in your spirit and gives purpose, meaning, and direction to your soul. His light brings health and well-being to your body. The Bible also says in Psalm 119:130,

> The entrance of thy words giveth light; it giveth understanding unto the simple.

Light is defined in this verse as understanding, and what brings understanding is the Word of God. It comes in and lights the candle, your spirit. The Word illuminates your spirit and brings revelation to your mind. The Holy Spirit, your Teacher, gives you understanding about who you are, what you were created to do in life, and divine guidance concerning every choice you make.

THE POWER OF CHOICE

When God called me into the ministry, He gave me understanding by lighting my spirit with an illustration. I saw a doctor's office with a lot of people walking by outside. The doctor was inside doing busy work, and he didn't put out his sign that said, "Open for Business." Then I saw all these people lined up outside his office just waiting for him to open up and treat them. The Holy Spirit spoke to my spirit, "Son, you've got to go into the ministry because a lot of people are waiting on what I have put in you."

God wants you to make the right decisions so that you can fulfill the destiny He has for you, and in the process a whole lot of other people will get touched and blessed by Him. But to make the right decisions you have to have revelation and understanding, which you will not get unless you renew your mind with God's Word.

Your soul is your mind, your emotions, and your will. It is where you make decisions. Therefore, your destiny and the quality of your life are determined by your soul. That is why the Bible stresses that you must be transformed by the renewing of your mind. You have to get your mind transformed by the Word of God, which means it comes under complete submission to the Holy Spirit in your spirit. Then you will begin to think, speak, and act like Jesus instead of that old selfish, sinful person you were before you got saved. You will act from your communication with God instead of your physical senses and carnal thinking. You will cease living the low life and live the high life!

Your soul is where the battle lies. Whoever and whatever controls your soul—whoever and whatever possesses your thinking, your emotions, and your will—determines the course of your life. This is something the enemy knows, and the devil and his demons will do everything they can to get your mind on anything but the Word of God.

Your life today is a result of the decisions you have made in the past. God gave you a free will and He will guard and protect it. He has such respect and regard for your free will that He will let you choose hell over Him in your lifetime. The enemy also knows this, and he will try to influence your decisions by capturing your soul.

The devil and his demons influence your decisions through circumstances and your physical environment. They introduce thoughts to your mind and get you focused on what your five physical senses perceive. They will use people they can influence to harm you or offend you. Some people have no idea they are being used by the enemy. They are either unbelievers or believers with unrenewed minds. They can think they are doing the right thing, but they are deceived.

A great example of someone who thought he was doing good was Saul of Tarsus, who later became the apostle Paul. Before he was saved he was responsible for the persecution and execution of Christians, and he believed he was faithfully serving God in doing this! Paul's life demonstrated how Satan influenced the decisions he made before he was saved, and Jesus influenced the decisions he made after he was saved. He went from living the low life to living the high life.

We live the low life under Satan, but we live the high life in Jesus Christ!

Unbelievers may not be aware of Satan's influence or even that they have the power of choice. As believers, however, we know from God's Word that God will always give us the final decision.

> I call heaven and earth to record this day against you, that I have set before you life and death, blessing and cursing: therefore choose life, that both thou and thy seed may live:
>
> Deuteronomy 30:19

Life is choice-driven, and your soul is where the choice to live or die is made.

Satan knows that whoever controls the soul of a person will control the experience and destiny of that person. He went into the Garden with the express purpose of becoming the influence over mankind. Because God had given Adam and Eve dominion over the Earth, the only way Satan could gain control of the Earth was to gain control of Adam and Eve.

When Adam turned from God's influence to Satan's influence, he sinned. And when Adam fell the whole human race fell. It is a lie from the devil that your sin affects only you! Your sin always affects the lives of everyone around you, just like Adam's sin affected all of us. If Satan can get just one person to do what he wants them to do, he can cause a whole lot of hurt in this world.

On the other hand, if God has all the influence in your life, He can do a whole lot of good in this world! As believers we need to keep our souls full of God and His Word. Then we will be making the right choices and have a godly impact on the world around us.

Whoever we trust with our lives is the one who will possess our soul, and whoever has our soul is going to influence our decisions and our destiny. We want God to completely possess our soul so that His good, acceptable, and perfect will can be proven in our lives. And when the people around us see all the love, peace, joy, and success we have, they will want to know Jesus and begin living the high life too.

I'm going to challenge you to check yourself throughout your day. From time to time just ask yourself, "Who's got my soul right now?" This will do two things. It will give the Holy Spirit the opportunity to expose any ungodly influence or thinking, and it will put you in remembrance of God's Word and will for your life. Just asking yourself that simple question can make the difference between success and failure, misery and happiness, and even life and death.

CHAPTER 2

DEFEATING THE ENEMY OF YOUR SOUL

Whoso keepeth his mouth and his tongue keepeth his soul from troubles.

Proverbs 21:23

The devil is your enemy! He is nothing but a trouble-maker, and this verse of Scripture is telling us that a key to keeping trouble away from our souls is to watch what comes out of our mouths. The enemy knows that he can do only what human beings give him permission to do. So if we speak trouble, we give him permission to make trouble.

If thou hast done foolishly in lifting up thyself, or if thou hast thought evil, lay thine hand upon thy mouth.

Proverbs 30:32

If you have a wrong thought, put your hand over your mouth. Don't speak it out! The enemy gave you that thought because he wants you to release it into the Earth. He wants you to grant him permission to do that evil thing.

> I said, I will take heed to my ways, that I sin not with my tongue: I will keep my mouth with a bridle, while the wicked is before me.
>
> Psalm 39:1

David lays it right on the line here. The devil is before him, introducing evil thoughts, and he is refusing to utter any of it. He will not speak evil.

Many times the devil is standing before people. They can't see him because he's a spirit, and he's waiting on authorization to do something terrible in the Earth. Because we have dominion over the Earth, he has to get our permission, which comes through our speech. So he tries to get us to speak the evil thought he gave us.

> Make no friendship with an angry man; and with a furious man thou shalt not go:
>
> Lest thou learn his ways, and get a snare to thy soul.
>
> Proverbs 22:24-25

An angry, furious person—someone who has allowed their offense or their hurt to rule their soul—cannot be your friend. If you hang around an individual who refuses to forgive, who will not submit to God's Word or His Spirit, then you are having fellowship with the enemy. You are opening your soul to be influenced by the devil.

God is letting you know where the danger to your soul lies. This is His wisdom. He is telling you this to keep you safe. Your angry friend is being used by the enemy to steal your destiny, your family, your money, and your heritage. If you receive and begin to speak the angry words of your friend, you will give the devil permission to wreak havoc in your life and other people's lives.

A lot of people think they know more than God. They think they can withstand the angry person. Or maybe it is the sexy person! Maybe it is the highly intelligent person. Maybe it is the person really gifted in sports or in the arts. But the enemy is using them to draw you away from God into his evil influence. If you are saved, you don't need to be dating and getting close to a person who is not saved. If you are married you don't need to be going out and partying after hours with people other than your spouse.

One of the first things you say is, "Well, I'm gonna get them saved." As a pastor I hear that all the time—especially after the tragedy. "Well, Pastor, I thought that if I went out with him and got close to him, then he would see Jesus' love in me and get saved. I never thought I would end up pregnant and alone like this." Or I hear, "Oh, Pastor, I wish I had never started going to that bar with the people I work with. I never thought I'd end up in a rehab center. I really thought I was going to get those people saved."

I'm not saying we should never associate with unbelievers. But let's have some wisdom in it! Unbelievers are not supposed to be our mates, our best friends, our business partners, our girlfriends, or our boyfriends. Who we have intimate contact with is a big part of guarding our souls. If we are to keep our minds renewed with the Word of God and live the high life, we must be wise when it comes to who we hang around, who we date, who we marry, who we live with, who we work with, and who we trust with our lives.

We can stay safe by continually asking ourselves, Who's got my soul?

FIERY TRIALS

Beloved, think it not strange concerning the fiery trial which is to try you, as though some strange thing happened unto you.

1 Peter 4:12

We are not to think it is strange when the enemy comes against us with fiery trials. We are not to see this as something unusual because he is evil and he doesn't like us. As a matter of fact, he hates us because we have dominion over the Earth and, as children of God, we bring the presence of God wherever we go. We release the power of the Holy Ghost and shut the devil out! If we see the devil or his demons doing something, in the authority of Jesus' name we get rid of them. Therefore, he is going to do everything he can do to stop us.

As a born-again child of God the devil has no spiritual hold on you anymore, but he still has access to your soul.

And your soul is where you make decisions. Therefore, he does everything he can to get control of your soul. If he can get control of your soul he can thwart the purposes of God in your life and affect the lives of everyone around you for evil instead of good.

There are many ways the enemy will come at you, and you need to guard your heart and mind from these strategies and traps. He can use other people or circumstances to snare you, but if you are not ignorant of his devices and your mind is renewed to the truth, you can keep from being deceived and led astray.

DISCOURAGEMENT

One of the powerful things the enemy uses to influence us is discouragement. God says throughout His Word that we are to have courage, and the opposite of courage is discouragement. The devil wants you to think that you don't have the strength or the ability to do what God has called you to do. He wants you to believe that you are worthless and hopeless when it comes to your marriage, your kids, your job, or whatever challenge you face.

Discouragement is not something that usually happens in a split second. It is sneaky. It creeps up on you slowly. The devil will introduce a negative thought one day then another negative thought the next. After about a week of meditating on all this negativity you begin to lose heart. You slow down. You are discouraged and you might not even realize it. All you know is you are sad and have no energy.

David showed us how to deal with discouragement. He came back from winning a big battle only to find that the enemy had burned the city of Ziklag, carried off his and his men's wives and children, and stolen all their possessions. Today it would be like coming in from a hard day's work to discover that somebody had stolen all the furniture in your house and had kidnapped your family. That would discourage you!

In David's situation, however, he faced not only the loss of his family and possessions, but also the wrath of his men. They began to take it out on David! They blamed him for everything and turned on him. Nobody was there to encourage David. He stood alone. No wife was there to lift him up. No children were there to love him unconditionally. He couldn't even watch Monday night football because his television was gone!

> David was greatly distressed; for the people spake of stoning him, because the soul of all the people was grieved, every man for his sons and for his daughters: *but David encouraged himself in the Lord his God.*
>
> 1 Samuel 30:6 (italics mine)

Sometimes you have to encourage yourself, and the only way to encourage yourself is in the Lord. Go to the Word of God. Get alone with God and say, "God, I need some encouragement. I don't have anyone here at the house.

Nobody in the church seems to be reaching out to me. It looks like things are going wrong at my job, and my supervisor doesn't understand what I'm trying to say. Lord, show me in Your Word what I need to think about all this. Give me some encouragement."

The great thing about turning to God for encouragement is that He will not only strengthen you and lift you up, but also He will give you wisdom on how to handle the situation or circumstances that have tried to discourage you.

When you go to the Lord for encouragement in His Word, you are putting yourself in position to be transformed!

> David enquired at the Lord, saying, Shall I pursue after this troop? shall I overtake them? And he answered him, Pursue: for thou shalt surely overtake them, and without fail recover all.
>
> 1 Samuel 30:8

David completely defeated discouragement by getting a word from the Lord. This word from God lit up his spirit and renewed his mind with the truth that if God is for you who can be against you (see Romans 8:31). As a result, the Bible says in 1 Samuel 30:18-19 that David and his men went out and recovered everyone and everything the enemy had stolen from them.

> David recovered all that the Amalekites had carried away: and David rescued his two wives.

And there was nothing lacking to them, neither small nor great, neither sons nor daughters, neither spoil, nor any thing that they had taken to them: David recovered all.

1 Samuel 30:18-19

The next time discouragement tries to capture your soul, stop it! Get your Bible, play a message on tape or CD, or turn on Christian television to get your mind renewed. Find out what God has to say about your situation. The Comforter will comfort you and teach you what you need to know to overcome and get the victory in that situation. You will be transformed!

PRESSURE

If the enemy cannot discourage you he will try to pressure you into doing what he wants you to do. He has always done this to the saints of God. In Daniel, chapter 3, he influenced King Nebuchadnezzar to build an image of himself and command the people to bow down and worship that image whenever music sounded. This was during the time of the Jewish captivity, and there were three Jewish boys—Shadrach, Meshach, and Abednego—who refused. They would bow only to and worship the God of Israel.

There were people in the king's court who were under the devil's influence and hated the children of God, so they ran to the king and said, "King, when the music sounds, Shadrach, Meschach, and Abednego don't bow or worship your image." The king immediately summoned the three boys.

Nebuchadnezzar spake and said unto them, Is it true, O Shadrach, Meshach, and Abednego, do not ye serve my gods, nor worship the golden image which I have set up?

Now if ye be ready that at what time ye hear the sound of the cornet, flute, harp, sackbut, psaltery, and dulcimer, and all kinds of musick, ye fall down and worship the image which I have made; well: but if ye worship not, ye shall be cast the same hour into the midst of a burning fiery furnace; and who is that God that shall deliver you out of my hands?

Daniel 3:14-15

This was certainly meant to put the pressure on these boys. Their lives were on the line. How did they answer the king?

Shadrach, Meshach, and Abednego, answered and said to the king, O Nebuchadnezzar, we are not careful to answer thee in this matter.

If it be so, our God whom we serve is able to deliver us from the burning fiery furnace, and he will deliver us out of thine hand, O king.

But if not, be it known unto thee, O king, that we will not serve thy gods, nor worship the golden image which thou hast set up.

Daniel 3:16-18

They said, "King, we don't even have to think about this. Our God will deliver us." Now don't misinterpret the Scripture. "But if not..." in verse 18 means, "If you don't throw us in there, we still won't bow." It does not mean, "If you do throw us in and God does not deliver us, we still won't bow." Obviously, if they burned up in the fire, bowing would no longer be an issue! This has been taught incorrectly, which encourages people to believe God will not always deliver them. But those boys had their minds renewed with God's promise of deliverance from any fire and flood, and they knew God would deliver them.

The enemy applied the pressure, but these boys did not waver in their faith. When you find yourself making a decision that is not of God just to relieve the pressure, you are making a decision for death and cursing instead of life and blessing. You are placing your life in the enemy's hands, and that always means more trouble and more pressure. Only by turning to the Word and the Spirit will you find the answers you need and the peace that passes all understanding.

When you speak and act on God's Word and the leading of His Spirit, you are choosing the high life and defeating pressure. The reason the three boys did not burn is because they did not bow to the pressure of the enemy. They knew who their real enemy was! They put their faith in God and His Word and nothing else, and they were able to do that because their minds were renewed.

The enemy will put pressure on you to run from your problems, get a divorce, leave your family, quit your job, or just lie down and quit. He will get you so afraid of the future, of your circumstances, and of the people in your life, you will run and hide. He is simply putting pressure on your mind to get you to make the decision he wants you to make. But God always provides a way of escape!

THE WAY OF ESCAPE

Thank God we are not without hope when the pressure seems unbearable. The very people who put pressure on us, who are under the influence of the enemy in the world, don't have the Holy Ghost. They don't have God's Word on the matter. They don't know the power of the Name and blood of Jesus. All they know is what their senses and their natural minds tell them, and most of those thoughts are from the devil.

Believers operate on a higher level of life. We live from our spirits because our minds are renewed with the truth of God's Word. We walk by the Spirit and not after the flesh. We walk by faith and not by sight, and we know that God's promises are true. One of those promises is that He will always provide a way to escape the traps and attacks of the enemy.

> There hath no temptation taken you but such as is common to man: but God is faithful, who will not suffer you to be tempted above that ye are able; but will with the temptation also make a way to escape, that ye may be able to bear it.
>
> 1 Corinthians 10:13

Remember, the enemy is after your soul. He wants you to go down a path of destruction, and he usually applies pressure to try to get you to make a quick decision. Then you won't take the time to consult the Word and the Spirit. But God promised you in writing that He's got a way of escape.

In every situation you might have pressure on you, but God has a way of escape.

When God makes a way of escape for you, and you follow His way, you will escape to a higher place. You will come out victorious. You won't be ashamed. On the other hand, if you succumb to the pressure, you will say, "I just can't take this anymore. I don't see any other way. I've just got to get out from underneath this pressure." Then you will sink to an even lower place.

What will help you to take God's way of escape? What will enable you to make decisions according to the Word and the Spirit of God?

> For though we walk in the flesh, we do not war after the flesh:
>
> (For the weapons of our warfare are not carnal, but mighty through God to the pulling down of strong holds;)
>
> Casting down imaginations, and every high thing that exalteth itself against the knowledge of God, and bringing into captivity every thought to the obedience of Christ.
>
> 2 Corinthians 10:3-5

I used to think this passage of Scripture meant we were supposed to go to the top of a mountain or the Sears Tower in Chicago and tell the devil where to go. But the strongholds here are in our minds! These are thought patterns and belief systems the enemy has programmed us with. He has filled our minds with thought patterns like, "I'm not good enough for God to bless me in this situation. I can't do what other people can do because of my past. I've always been afraid of that and I always will be afraid of that. I'm weak. That's just the way I am. I'll never change."

You can go to your Bible and pull those strongholds down in your mind. Read about who you are in Christ Jesus. It says in 2 Corinthians 5:17 that you are a new creature, a new species of being. It also says that your past has passed! You are new, and your past is gone forever. Renew your mind with the truth! Start thinking and saying, "I'm brand new. My whole life is new. My past is no longer going to cause me to live the low life. Jesus has brought me into the high life."

BRAND NEW MEANS BRAND NEW

One of the enemy's biggest strategies to keep control of our soul is guilt, shame, and condemnation about our past, the times we've fallen, and the times we've failed. That is why it is crucial that we renew our minds to what God thinks and feels about us as His children.

When you came into the Kingdom of God, your body may not have changed. You were still fat or skinny or the right weight. But inside you were brand new! The person who did all that sinning in your past was dead. Glory to God! Now you live according to your spirit instead of your flesh. And you no longer have a desire to sin.

The woman caught in the midst of adultery had every reason to feel dirty, guilty, and unworthy. But Jesus had some interesting things to say about her. He turned to the religious people and said, "He that is without sin among you, let him first cast a stone at her" (John 8:7). One by one they threw down their rocks and walked away. Then Jesus turned to the woman and said, "Woman, where are your accusers? Has any man condemned you?"

She said, "I don't see any."

He said, "I don't condemn you either. Go and sin no more" (see vv. 10-11).

Jesus never condemns. He saves, heals, and restores.

God sent not his Son into the world to condemn the world; but that the world through him might be saved.

John 3:17

God isn't going to bring up your past because it's passed! It passed away when you were born again. The way of escape from haunting memories always begins with renewing the mind to God's truth about you. You are forgiven. You are cleansed. He whom the Son has set free is free indeed (see John 8:36).

Whenever the enemy tries to paint you into a corner with discouragement and pressure and guilt, purge those evil thoughts and bad memories by washing your mind with God's holy Word. This is the power of your salvation! The Word of God will flood your soul with the reality of righteousness, peace, and joy in the Holy Ghost until any guilt, shame, fear, doubt, rage, or loneliness will disappear altogether.

Just ask the apostle Paul about being brand new. As Saul of Tarsus he hauled Christian men and women to jail, their children crying as he dragged their parents out to be executed. That is how mean religion is. Then he got saved and realized what he had done. So God had to give him a revelation of righteousness, peace, and joy in the Holy Ghost, or he would never have been able to hold up his head or do anything for God. He got his mind renewed to being a new creature, and he was able to say,

> Receive us; we have wronged no man, we have corrupted no man, we have defrauded no man.
>
> 2 Corinthians 7:2

This is the same man who persecuted and murdered Christians! Paul had fully embraced the truth that he was a new creature in Christ Jesus and all those old things had been washed away by Jesus' blood—never to be brought up again.

Having a renewed mind will stop the devil in his tracks. If he comes up behind you and catches you unawares, you can go to God and His Word and get your mind more renewed! You have at your disposal God's weapons of spiritual warfare that are mighty and always victorious. So don't let the enemy capture your soul and steal your inheritance in Christ Jesus. Keep your mind renewed with God's Word and you will defeat the enemy of your soul every time he tries one of his evil tricks.

CHAPTER 3

YOU CAN'T GO WHERE YOU CAN'T SEE

When I was a little boy I used to go to horror movies on Saturday. My brother and I would sit in the theater and watch two or three of them. *Wolfman* and *Wolfman's Mama*…whatever was playing. That night my brother and I would get in our bunk beds, our dad would turn out the light, and my thoughts would be filled with all that I had seen that day at the movies.

My brother would wait until the lights were out and it was quiet, then he would begin to moan, "Oooooo…oooooo…oooooo." I'd try to ignore him and act like it didn't bother me, but after awhile my imagination would kick in. It wasn't long before I was sure the Wolfman was in the room, breathing down on me, and my body would begin to shake. Pretty soon I would cry out, "Daddy!" and he'd come in and give us both a whipping!

My imagination was filled with pictures of that scary Wolfman. Therefore, the enemy had my soul, and destruction followed! I was frozen with fear, cried out in terror, and got a whipping on top of all that. This is generally what happens when the enemy captures your imagination. We know from 2 Corinthians 10:5 that there are vain (empty, futile, and sometimes evil) imaginations that we are to cast down. But God gave us our imagination, which means He has a purpose for it.

THE MYTH OF ORIGINAL THOUGHT

Our imagination is the part of our mind where we can visualize something that is not manifest in the physical world around us. We can imagine something based on a previous experience or acquired knowledge, such as when I imagined Wolfman standing over me in my bedroom. That imagination was based on a prior experience.

Our imagination can also be a vision or revelation from God. If our minds are renewed with His Word and we are following Him, the Holy Spirit can communicate with us through our imagination. We have the ability to see by the Spirit things that do not yet exist, experiences we have not experienced, and ideas we have never encountered.

The world believes that a person's imagination is the source of their individual creativity, the place of "original thought." However, the Bible tells us that human beings were created to live in relationship with the Lord. He is our

Source of life and all knowledge. Therefore, we have no original thoughts. We receive information and revelation from the Holy Spirit and God's Word—or from the enemy. We either serve the Lord or we serve Satan. We make decisions based upon our spiritual relationship with God or our carnal, natural connection to the enemy.

The fact that we have no original thought offends the pride of people who don't know the Lord because they like to believe their ideas are their own. Most of them have no idea there is a devil and demons out there that are feeding them thoughts and images, programming their minds and influencing them to do what they want them to do. But everything we think causes our imaginations to be filled with ideas and mental images that were put there by either the Holy Spirit or the enemy.

> For by him [Jesus] were all things created, that are in heaven, and that are in earth, visible and invisible, whether they be thrones, or dominions, or principalities, or powers: all things were created by him, and for him:
> And he is before all things, and by him all things consist.
>
> Colossians 1:16-17 (brackets mine)

All things means all things. Every creature and every molecule of the physical and spiritual realms was created by Jesus. But also, every thought, idea, or mental image was created by Him. All the enemy can do is take what Jesus created and pervert it, bend it, and distort it into something wicked and deceptive. The devil has no original thoughts! Only God is capable of original thought.

I know what you're thinking. *Well, Pastor, are you saying I'm just a robot that is programmed by God or the devil?* No. You are programmable, but your programming is subject to your will. Remember, God gave you free will. You choose your programming. You decide what goes in and what is cast off in your imagination and thought life. Furthermore, you were created for fellowship with Him. Your life is led in relationship with your Heavenly Father, and a relationship involves communication, intimacy, discussion, and mutual decision. You are not a robot; you are a son or daughter of God.

WITHOUT A VISION...

Where there is no vision, the people perish: but he that keepeth the law, happy is he.

Proverbs 29:18

The first part of this verse of Scripture is quoted all the time, but I want you to notice something. If you read the whole verse, vision and happiness are both linked directly to the Word of God. Those who keep the law are happy. They are happy because they abide in God's Word, which enlightens their minds and gives them vision for their lives. Then they can see where they are to go. You cannot go where you cannot see!

Shadrach, Meschach, and Abednego meditated in God's Word day and night. That's why they had a steadfast faith that He would deliver them from Nebuchadnezzar's fiery furnace. And God did deliver them. However, if they had sat in front of their television sets all day and all night, we might be reading a different story in the Bible today! "Television" is something "telling" you its "vision." You are receiving a vision for your life, and in most cases it is probably not something from God. If you want to be able to live through the fiery furnaces of life, you better make sure that what you are seeing is God's vision for your life.

Joseph had a vision from God that came through dreams. A dream is another way in which God can impart vision to our lives.

> Joseph dreamed a dream, and he told it his brethren: and they hated him yet the more.
>
> And he said unto them, Hear, I pray you, this dream which I have dreamed:
>
> For, behold, we were binding sheaves in the field, and, lo, my sheaf arose, and also stood upright; and, behold, your sheaves stood round about, and made obeisance to my sheaf.
>
> And his brethren said to him, Shalt thou indeed reign over us? or shalt thou indeed have dominion over us? And they hated him yet the more for his dreams, and for his words.
>
> And he dreamed yet another dream, and told it his brethren, and said, Behold, I have dreamed a dream more; and, behold, the sun and the moon and the eleven stars made obeisance to me.
>
> Genesis 37:5-9

Through this dream God painted a vivid picture on Joseph's mind that one day his family and nations would bow down to him. When he shared these dreams with his family, Joseph began a journey of ups and downs, defeat and victory, until finally the Word of the Lord was fulfilled in his life.

Even though Joseph went through a whole series of terrible trials and unjust circumstances—he remembered where he was going and never stopped believing. He chose to believe that what God had imprinted in his mind as a boy would surely come to pass. He chose that vision, that dream, again and again until it finally came to pass.

Joseph understood he would go to the place he could see.

God also imparts vision through the natural creation around us. This is how He showed Abram the land He had given him and his descendants.

> The Lord said unto Abram, after that Lot was separated from him, Lift up now thine eyes, and look from the place where thou art northward, and southward, and eastward, and westward:
>
> For all the land which thou seeth, to thee will I give it, and to thy seed for ever.
>
> Genesis 13:14-15

God said to Abram, "If you can see it, you can have it." He didn't mean just with the natural eye. He also was talking about seeing with our spiritual eyes. If we can see it in the spirit, what the Word of God promises us, and our minds grab hold of the God-given image, we can have it.

What we are talking about is divine revelation and vision that bring forth our divine destiny.

See It, Believe It, Do It, Have It

The whole earth was of one language, and of one speech.

And it came to pass, as they journeyed from the east, that they found a plain in the land of Shinar; and they dwelt there.

And they said one to another, Go to, let us make brick, and burn them thoroughly. And they had brick for stone, and slime had they for morter.

And they said, Go to, let us build us a city and a tower, whose top may reach unto heaven; and let us make us a name, lest we be scattered abroad upon the face of the whole earth.

And the Lord came down to see the city and the tower, which the children of men builded.

And the Lord said, Behold, the people is one, and they have all one language; and this they begin to do: *and now nothing will be restrained from them, which they have imagined to do.*

Genesis 11:1-6 (italics mine)

These people did not worship and serve God, so He stopped them from completing their tower by confusing their languages (see verse 7) and scattering them throughout the Earth (see verse 8). However, we can see that their imaginations were extremely powerful. What their minds could conceive they could have. This is true with unbelievers as well as believers because it is the way God created human beings.

In order to prove God's will, we want to make certain our imaginations are stimulated by Him alone. In the following story, we see again how God used His creation to implant His vision for Abram in Abram's imagination.

> After these things the word of the Lord came unto Abram in a vision, saying, Fear not, Abram: I am thy shield, and thy exceeding great reward.
>
> And Abram said, Lord God, what wilt thou give me, seeing I go childless, and the steward of my house is this Eliezer of Damascus?
>
> And Abram said, Behold, to me thou hast given no seed: and, lo, one born in my house is mine heir.
>
> And, behold, the word of the Lord came unto him, saying, This shall not be thine heir; but he that shall come forth out of thine own bowels shall be thine heir.
>
> And he brought him forth abroad, and said, Look now toward heaven, and tell the stars, if thou be able to number them: and he said unto him, So shall thy seed be.
>
> And he believed in the Lord; and he counted it to him for righteousness.
>
> Genesis 15:1-6

What did God do to stimulate Abram's imagination? He brought him outside and told him to count the stars. Abram responded by saying, "There are too many. I can't count them."

God answered, "That's how many kids you're going to have." From that moment on Abram saw more than stars in the sky. Every night he looked toward the heavens and saw his future, his divine destiny. He saw it. He believed it. He moved toward it. And therefore he eventually saw it come to pass.

One of the things I want you to notice here is that when you receive revelation, vision, and imaginations from God—they are always big! In fact, they will always be too big and too impossible for you to accomplish in your own abilities and strength. But God knows what you can handle, and He gives you His Word so you can handle the rest by having faith in Him.

> Now to Him Who, by (in consequence of) the [action of His] power that is at work within us, is able to [carry out His purpose and] do superabundantly, far over and above all that we [dare] ask or think [infinitely beyond our highest prayers, desires, thoughts, hopes, or dreams] to Him be glory.
>
> Ephesians 3:20-21 AMP

You can't think big enough for God! He wants to stimulate your imagination more than you ever could in your lifetime. You are hooked up with a God who wants to do great and mighty works through you, but He's got to get you to see it and believe it so you can do it. He has to impart His vision to your imagination so that you can have everything He wants you to have. And He does that primarily through His Word, as you renew your mind and meditate on it. He also gives you visions, dreams, and speaks through His natural, material creation. Then, as you meditate and renew your mind with His promises, you can move forward to possess them.

SEEING THE IMPOSSIBLE MAKES IT POSSIBLE

When you are born again, your potential is no longer limited to yourself. Your potential is in God. Your potential goes beyond your natural abilities and gifts into His supernatural authority and power. However, until you were saved you were programmed to believe you had natural limitations and boundaries. You believed you could do only what you could naturally think and do. When God puts it in your heart to do something impossible, if you still believe you are limited to your natural abilities and gifts, you will back up and not move.

I have news for you. God will never call you to do something you are entirely incapable of doing, but He will enable you to do it supernaturally. There never was a better example of this than when the children of Israel went to the Promised Land for the first time. Moses sent twelve spies in to see just what they were getting into.

They returned from searching of the land after forty days.

And they went and came to Moses, and to Aaron, and to all the congregation of the children of Israel, unto the wilderness of Paran, to Kadesh; and brought back word unto them, and unto all the congregation, and shewed them the fruit of the land.

And they told him, and said, We came unto the land whither thou sentest us, and surely it floweth with milk and honey; and this is the fruit of it.

Nevertheless the people be strong that dwell in the land, and the cities are walled, and very great: and moreover we saw the children of Anak there.

The Amalekites dwell in the land of the south: and the Hittites, and the Jebusites, and the Amorites, dwell in the mountains: and the Canaanites dwell by the sea, and by the coast of Jordan.

And Caleb stilled the people before Moses, and said, Let us go up at once, and possess it; for we are well able to overcome it.

Numbers 13:25-30

Of the twelve spies, only Joshua and Caleb came back and said, "Let's go right now and possess what God has already given us. We can do it because He said we could do it." This is the kind of leadership God always looks for. The world will say, "Ah, you win some and you lose some." But God says, "I always cause you to triumph in Christ Jesus!" (see 2 Corinthians 2:14.) Our victory is already won because Jesus already won it.

Every battle you fight you can win if you will keep your mind renewed with the truth of God's Word. "But, Pastor, you don't know how much opposition I'm facing. There are giants!" If there are giants, then God has given you the means of defeating them. He has put His Spirit and Word inside you, and you know you are supposed to fight and win this battle. You know you are supposed to be a winner and not a quitter—you have an inheritance in Jesus Christ to possess.

When I found out about my inheritance, I said, "Wait a minute! Those giants are sitting on my stuff! That land belongs to me." If the children of Israel had lined up their imaginations and thoughts with God, they would have realized that He had had those giants prepare everything for them. Those big guys had built beautiful houses with atriums and gardens, and they had plowed the fields and had grown all kinds of wonderful fruits and vegetables to eat. God used those giants to prepare everything for His children!

The problem was, the children of Israel did not see their potential in God, and they did not see the giants as God saw them. Instead, they had a grasshopper image of themselves and saw those giants annihilating them.

> The men that went up with him said, We be not able to go up against the people; for they are stronger than we.
>
> And they brought up an evil report of the land which they had searched unto the children of Israel, saying, The land, through which we have gone to search it, is a land that eateth up the inhabitants thereof; and all the people that we saw in it are men of a great stature.
>
> And there we saw the giants, the sons of Anak, which come of the giants: and we were in our own sight as grasshoppers, and so we were in their sight.
>
> Numbers 13:31-33

The other ten spies brought back an evil report. They measured their lives by their natural abilities instead of God's Word and power. They saw themselves as grasshoppers, and God called that *evil.*

I had a similar experience when God called me to quit my job and go into full-time ministry. I had a great job that paid well and had good benefits. I had a family, a mortgage, and the cars to pay for. All my bills seemed like giants to me. How could I quit my job and go into the ministry? That was where my thinking was at that time. My imagination was filled with pictures of me ministering full time in failure, poverty, and defeat.

I began to wrestle with these images in my mind. The Holy Spirit was telling me to leave that job! In desperation I began to meditate this verse of Scripture:

> Jesus answered and said, Verily I say unto you, There is no man that hath left house, or brethren, or sisters, or father, or mother, or wife, or children, or lands, for my sake, and the gospel's,
>
> But he shall receive an hundredfold now in this time, houses, and brethren, and sisters, and mothers, and children, and lands, with persecutions; and in the world to come eternal life.
>
> Mark 10:29-30

Now I began to question the limitations and boundaries the world had placed on me. The more I meditated on and thought according to the Word of God, the less I was manipulated by old, ungodly thinking. I began to see myself prosperous and fulfilled as a minister of the Gospel. The day came when I had such a clear picture in my mind of how fantastic it would be to serve God in full-time ministry that ministry was all I wanted to do. I became completely dissatisfied with my job even though it was a good job and everyone treated me right. One day I just picked up the phone, called my wife, and said, "I'm quitting my job!"

She said, "Well, praise the Lord!" God had already prepared her heart, and we were in agreement that it was time to take that step of faith. I shudder to think what might have happened if I had not meditated on God's Word and never allowed Him to change the picture I had of His faithfulness and my potential in Him. You see, I could not go where I could not see!

From this day on, let God fill your imagination and thought-life with His Word and His will for your life. Choose to be programmed by Him instead of the world around you and the enemy behind it. I promise you that you will be able to move forward in all He's called you to do with supernatural wisdom and ability you never dreamed possible. One day you will wake up and look back to see all the things you have accomplished and marvel that everything God showed you in your heart, with the eyes of your spirit, came to pass.

CHAPTER 4

LEAVING YOUR COMFORT ZONE

If we are going to follow Jesus, we are going to move out of our comfort zone again and again. The Bible guarantees it. So let's first take a look at what our comfort zone is. How do we get into a comfort zone in the first place?

We have seen that the enemy is after our soul. The soul is the mind, emotions, and will; and he tries to influence our decisions by introducing thoughts and pressuring us with circumstances. Then we saw that what we can see from God's Word we can have. If we can imagine it and believe it, we can have it. We can do what God says we can do if we can see ourselves doing it. That's why the devil tries to capture our minds. Whatever occupies our mind—what we see and believe in our soul—is going to determine our destiny.

If we want to experience God's perfect will and fulfill His purpose in our lives, we must make right choices, and our choices are made from the strongest images and thoughts in our minds. The enemy will always try to create a comfort zone based upon images and thoughts that are contrary to what the Word of God says about us. He gets us to continue making bad decisions because we are stuck in that comfort zone.

One of the reasons we do not make the right decisions is because of our past experiences. We may be born again, but our past is still affecting our choices. That's where renewing our minds becomes vital. When we renew our minds with God's Word, we are literally renovating our belief system, our patterns of thought, our imagination, and our emotions to come out of an ungodly comfort zone into a godly comfort zone. We are turning from the low life, living disconnected from God, to the high life—living as a child of God.

REPROGRAMMING OUR BELIEFS

If we didn't get saved as young children, or we were saved but were not taught to keep our minds renewed in God's Word, we probably have been programmed by the enemy. Therefore, to live the high life in Jesus Christ we need to enter into the process of reprogramming and retraining the way we think, imagine, speak, and act. We begin by recognizing that many of the things we have seen and heard and learned in the past came from the world systems and the enemies of God.

For example, the world tells you that as you get older you will have serious health problems like arthritis and loss of memory. You will run out of energy and creativity and retire at age sixty-five. But that's not what the Bible says. People who love and serve God do not grow old like that. Moses didn't lead the children of Israel out of Egypt until he was over eighty years old, and when he died his "eye was not dim, nor his natural force abated" (Deuteronomy 34:7). Moses was on the job until he died, and he didn't die because of sickness. He just went to heaven when God said, "It's time."

Consider Abraham and Sarah. Genesis 17:17 tells us that Sarah was ten years younger than Abraham. When they went down to Egypt and Pharaoh wanted to take Sarah into his harem, Abraham was seventy-five years old. That means Sarah was sixty-five, but Abraham said, "Tell the Egyptians you're my sister because, Baby, you're too good lookin', and that Pharaoh will want to kill me if he knows you're my wife." Now we know Pharaoh wasn't taking any women into his harem that didn't look fine! The girl had something going at sixty-five!

Abraham did all right too. After Sarah died, Genesis 25 tells us that Abraham took another wife and had more children. He was over 120 years old! This is not just an Old Testament phenomenon. There is no mention that any of the first apostles died sick. Church history tells us that they were all executed except John, and John was a vital participant in the church until he went to Heaven.

If you have been programmed by the world to believe you will struggle with all the curses and diseases your family has had, that you will get the flu when all your neighbors get the flu, and that you will die sick, then you need to renew your mind to get some God-given beliefs. You need to renovate that old, stinkin' thinkin' with the Word of God.

> Christ hath redeemed us from the curse of the law, being made a curse for us: for it is written, Cursed is every one that hangeth on a tree:
>
> That the blessing of Abraham might come on the Gentiles through Jesus Christ; that we might receive the promise of the Spirit through faith.
>
> Galatians 3:13-14

You do not have to have the sicknesses and diseases your family has had because your spiritual father is Abraham, and Abraham was not sick. He lived a long, productive life. Christ has redeemed us from the curse and all that's under the curse, which includes sickness and dying too soon. You have the blessing of Abraham! You don't have to retire at sixty-five. You don't have to have the flu or arthritis or cancer. But to live this high life you have to leave your comfort zone, the old ways of thinking and believing. Because you are what you think, then leaving your comfort zone means first changing what you think and believe.

LOOKING AT THE MIND

God created our minds with a conscious and a subconscious. The conscious part sees and knows what's going on. When we are conscious we are aware and knowledgeable. Our conscious mind reasons, calculates, and makes decisions. The subconscious part of us is fed by what the conscious part receives, and after repeating this input again and again, it establishes a set point or standard by which we operate unconsciously. For example, our conscious mind is in full control when we learn to ride a bike. However, after we have ridden a bike successfully for a certain length of time, our conscious mind doesn't think about how to ride that bike anymore. We just get on the bike and start pedalling without thinking about it. It is automatic because what was conscious has become subconscious through repetition.

The same process governs every other behavior pattern in our lives. What has been programmed into our subconscious is what we will say and do automatically given certain circumstances and stimuli. We could say that the subconscious is our autopilot, if you will. In an airplane, when the autopilot is engaged it keeps the airplane at a designated altitude and moving in a designated direction. If you turn off the autopilot and then turn it on again, the airplane will automatically go to the previously set altitude and direction unless you reprogram it. It is automatic.

Most of what we say and do is based on automatic programming of the subconscious. We awake and go through a morning routine without thinking about it. We do a large part of our jobs on autopilot, without consciously thinking about it. And when it is time to drive a car, do the dishes, swim, or play a piece of music we have played many times on the piano, we can be thinking consciously of something else while doing these things. This is the power of the subconscious in our lives.

The subconscious mind is automatic unless we change its programming. It was created so we wouldn't have to learn things over and over again. Once we learn how to ride a bicycle, we know how to ride it forever. When it's time to ride a bike, we just ride it. We don't think about it because the process has been written in our subconscious. How do we get something written into our subconscious? This happens either through repetition, as we experienced in riding a bike, or through an intense emotional experience.

The most intense emotional experience—whether or not it seems so at the time—is being born again. When we are born again we are redeemed from sin. All our sins are washed away forever by the blood of Jesus Christ. We are no longer going to hell with the lake of fire looming in our eternal future. We are going to Heaven to live with our loving Heavenly Father for eternity. Now that is emotional! Changing your eternal address will rock your world and shake up your comfort zone!

However emotional or unemotional our new birth experience is, the fact remains that our spirits are reborn but our souls are not. Although we have no desire to sin or displease God anymore, our minds (conscious and subconscious) have been programmed to think, speak, and act like the world and the enemy. So we must renew our minds with God's Word to begin to reap the full benefits of our salvation, think and act like Jesus, and receive our inheritance as His joint-heir.

REPROGRAMMING OUR AUTOPILOT

The Bible tells us how to reprogram our minds, and this applies to both our conscious and subconscious.

I beseech you therefore, brethren, by the mercies of God, that ye present your bodies a living sacrifice, holy, acceptable unto God, which is your reasonable service.

And be not conformed to this world: but be ye transformed by the renewing of your mind, that ye may prove what is that good, and acceptable, and perfect, will of God.

Romans 12:1-2

We are to read, study, meditate, and live according to the Word of God. This is how we reprogram ourselves to live like Jesus instead of the devil, to live the high life of the Kingdom of God instead of the low life of this world.

Be ye doers of the word, and not hearers only, deceiving your own selves.

> For if any be a hearer of the word, and not a doer, he is like unto a man beholding his natural face in a glass:
>
> For he beholdeth himself, and goeth his way, and straightway forgetteth what manner of man he was.
>
> James 1:22-24

The Greek word translated *glass* means "mirror."[1] The next verse tells us what our mirror is.

> But whoso looketh into the perfect law of liberty, and continueth therein, he being not a forgetful hearer, but a doer of the work, this man shall be blessed in his deed.
>
> James 1:25

The mirror we need to be looking into is the Word of God. Then we will be blessed in everything we do because we will see ourselves as God sees us. One of the first things we have to reprogram in our minds is the way we see ourselves.

When you get up in the morning and look at yourself in your natural mirror, do you like what you see? Usually not. So you immediately begin to straighten yourself up. You brush your teeth. You comb your hair. If you are a woman you put on some make-up. If you are a man you probably shave. You change the way you look by looking in that mirror.

The same holds true when we look in the mirror of the Word of God. We read about Jesus telling the disciples to forgive seventy times seven, and we remember how offended we were by something our boss said yesterday. Our mirror is telling us that we need to make an adjustment. We need to forgive and make right what was wrong and out of place. That old comfort zone of resentment and bitterness is no longer comfortable! God has given us a new comfort zone called forgiveness and unconditional love.

> We all, with open face beholding as in a glass the glory of the Lord, are changed into the same image from glory to glory, even as by the Spirit of the Lord.
>
> 2 Corinthians 3:18

We are supposed to look in the Word and get changed and conformed to the image of Christ Jesus. Every day we should look into the Word of God and identify ourselves more and more with Jesus and less and less with the world. We have been designed to operate just like God. Hallelujah!

The interesting thing about being transformed by the Word of God is that it affects the physical body. Remember when I went to the horror movies and my imagination was captured by all those frightening images? It affected my body. My body didn't know that what I was seeing in my imagination wasn't real. So I was trembling. I couldn't sleep. My heart was racing. My breathing was fast and shallow. I was not at ease. When I did finally go to sleep, I had scary dreams because I had allowed my subconscious to be programmed by horror movies. That was not living the high life!

To sleep peacefully and live in ease instead of dis-ease, I had to reprogram myself with God's Word. Disease is named that for a reason. It is dis-ease. When we are not at ease in our minds, when our imaginations are filled with all kinds of ungodly pictures and images, our bodies start acting like what we are thinking. However, when our minds are filled with the love and revelation of the Father who loves us, protects us, and provides for us, we are at ease. We have peace that passes all understanding. "The joy of the Lord is our strength" (Nehemiah 8:10). And our bodies are healthy and whole. That is the result of reprogramming our "autopilot" subconscious and our conscious mind with God's Word.

God's comfort zone is found in the truth of His Word.

REPLACING LIES WITH TRUTH

Then said Jesus to those Jews which believed on him, If ye continue in my word, then are ye my disciples indeed;
And ye shall know the truth, and the truth shall make you free.

John 8:31-32

We all want to be free, and the truth is the only thing that will get us free and keep us free. The Bible tells us that knowing the truth comes only one way: believing on Jesus and abiding in His Word. Then we can call ourselves disciples and we will be free. I hear all the time, "Well, Pastor, I just don't have time to spend in the Word. I'm starting a new business. I just had a baby. I'm running to all my children's activities. I've got too many things going on."

There is a way which seemeth right unto a man, but the end thereof are the ways of death.

Proverbs 14:12

Guess what? Our way can seem like the best way and still get us killed! Without the light of the Word of God shining in our hearts and minds, we don't know where we are going. We don't have a clue, in fact. And the best way to end up in bondage or a ditch somewhere is to neglect the renewing of our minds with God's Word.

The devil knows this, and he does something really interesting. He will see to it that believers get distracted and deceived away from God's Word, but he will tell unbelievers God's principles for success. He'll leave out that it's the Word of God. He won't talk about Jesus, His death on the Cross, or His resurrection. And he certainly won't speak of sin and redemption through Jesus' blood. However, he will make sure the people he wants to exalt in this world know just enough truth to be successful in what they do. You see, God's Word works whether or not you know or believe it is His Word.

When I teach organization and time management, there's no better place to teach it than out of the Bible. Here's a verse we have touched on, and it covers every area of our lives.

As he thinketh in his heart, so is he.

Proverbs 23:7

This is God's truth. Think evil and it will soon bring you to complete destruction. Think whatsoever things are true, honest, just, pure, lovely, of good report; and virtuous, and you will walk in peace (see Philippians 4:8-9). Remember, you will always move in the direction of your most dominant thoughts. Every successful businessman knows this truth!

> The rich man's wealth is his strong city: the destruction of the poor is their poverty.
>
> Proverbs 10:15

Why is the destruction of the poor their poverty? Because they think about it all the time! They wake up in the morning thinking about how they are going to pay the bills. They go to bed thinking about how much food they can buy. They need to believe on Jesus and continue in His Word. They need to see who they are in Him in the mirror of God's Word and change their programming.

Change your thoughts and you will change your life.

"Well, Pastor, you don't know what he did to me. You don't know the mess I'm in. You don't know how bad it is at work. You have no idea what I'm facing every morning." You better stop thinking those thoughts if you want to live the high life. What you're thinking is not good. It's not lovely. It's not a good report. I can look at some folks' faces and tell what they're thinking, can't you?

When we were little boys, my brother and I would start horsing around and making noise as soon as our mother got on the phone. She would look at us and the look on her face said, "Stop, or I'm going to get you!" Her face revealed all to us!

What you think and believe will show on the outside of you. You will speak and act according to your comfort zone, whether that was programmed by God or the devil. You will move in the direction of what you think and believe and make decisions from that point of reference. Therefore, if you want to set your autopilot on God's will and timing, you must renew your mind with His Word.

DOES THE TRUTH HURT?

I will not mislead you. Change involves some discomfort. What you have believed about yourself—that you're a worm with a criminal past and never get a break, that you're not smart enough or good-looking enough to succeed, that you don't have the talent or the drive other people have, or that you will never be able to have a happy family or healthy relationships—has given you an excuse to back off, quit, and fail. That kind of thinking is right from the pit of hell and has kept you from being who God created you to be, but it has been all you've ever known, and it has become your comfort zone.

Now God wants you to change. First, He wants you to change the way you see yourself. He wants you to see your-self as He sees you: righteous, holy, beloved of God, with a divine nature and destiny, endowed with His authority and power, full of His love and grace. Then He wants you to act like what you see. He wants you to be Jesus to everyone you meet and step out in faith to do what He's called you to do. Can you see how all this is impossible without renewing your mind with God's Word?

If you have dragged your feet with God, it's time to step up to the plate and get your mind renewed! Reprogram your conscious and subconscious mind with the Living Word and be healed in soul and body. Leave your old, worldly comfort zone behind and move into the high life with Jesus. Once you begin to walk in this life of His love, grace, and peace, you will never look back!

CHAPTER 5

LEARNING TO THINK RIGHT

I beseech you therefore, brethren, by the mercies of God, that ye present your bodies a living sacrifice, holy, acceptable unto God, which is your reasonable service.

And be not conformed to this world: but be ye transformed by the renewing of your mind, that ye may prove what is that good, and acceptable, and perfect, will of God.

Romans 12:1-2

This is written to the brethren, the brothers and sisters, which means you and me. And apparently our bodies have a purpose. We are to use them in the service of God, and what God is asking is totally reasonable. It is reasonable because Jesus died for us and redeemed us from eternal death and hell, so we have no problem serving Him with our whole being. Then, as we serve Him, we are never to forget Him as our example. We are not to be conformed to the world around us, to be squeezed into that mold or continue in ungodly behavior. Instead, we are to be transformed in a process like metamorphosis by renewing our minds with God's Word. The Word of God will renovate our thinking and thus transform our behavior to be as much like Jesus on the outside as the inside.

SPIRITUAL RENOVATION

The process of renovation is an interesting one. As I mentioned before, you tear out some walls, replace the plumbing and electrical wiring, and completely redecorate. Moreover, you add appliances, furniture, and conveniences that you have never used before. The basic structure is there, but everything contained in that structure is brand new. The same thing happens when we are born again. Our body is the basic structure, and then the Great Decorator, the Holy Spirit, moves in. He brings the life of God into our spirits, and the first thing He tells us is, "The past is gone. This is a new day, and you are a new person."

> Therefore if any man be in Christ, he is a new creature: old things are passed away; behold, all things are become new.
>
> 2 Corinthians 5:17

This is talking about our spirits. Although our soul (mind, emotions, will) is affected by this miracle transformation, it has not been transformed. So the Great Decorator begins to tear out old habits of thinking and behaving that are contrary to the truth of God's Word. The result is that we change. We begin to prove the good, acceptable, and perfect will of God to ourselves and everyone around us.

What I have just described is leaving the low life (living for ourselves, according to our senses and natural thinking) for the high life (living for Jesus, according to the Word and the Spirit). After the new birth we operate on an entirely different level, a spiritual level. We still remember our past and have the same thoughts. The ungodly patterns are still there. But now we have no desire to continue in them. A revolution has taken place inside us. Our spirits have rejected Satan's rule and surrendered completely to the Lord Jesus Christ. Now our soul and body have to line up with this revolutionary spiritual change—and the process of renovation begins.

God created our body to be submitted to our soul, and our soul to be submitted to our spirit, which is submitted to the Lord. We were created to love and work with Him. When we are born again, we are restored to that original purpose.

> Then will I sprinkle clean water upon you, and ye shall be clean: from all your filthiness, and from all your idols, will I cleanse you.
>
> A new heart also will I give you, and a new spirit will I put within you: and I will take away the stony heart out of your flesh, and I will give you an heart of flesh.
>
> And I will put my spirit within you, and cause you to walk in my statutes, and ye shall keep my judgments, and do them.
>
> Ezekiel 36:25-27

This passage of Scripture tells us that when we get born again we will be able to do everything God asks us to do in the New Covenant. We can walk in His statutes, keep His judgments, and obey His Word and will. We can do them! That means that everything in our lives will be changed for the better.

> Thus saith the Lord God; In the day that I shall have cleansed you from all your iniquities I will also cause you to dwell in the cities, and the wastes shall be builded.
>
> And the desolate land shall be tilled, whereas it lay desolate in the sight of all that passed by.
>
> And they shall say, This land that was desolate is become like the garden of Eden; and the waste and desolate and ruined cities are become fenced, and are inhabited.
>
> Ezekiel 36:33-35

These verses describe the renovation and restoration process that happens in our souls and bodies after we are born again and begin to renew our minds. Apart from God our lives were desolate and unfruitful, but now that we have been redeemed and restored to Him as our Lord and Savior, the whole landscape is changing. We are beginning to look like the Garden of Eden! When unbelievers are around us, they sense there is a higher level of life available to them. And why is all this happening? Because we are thinking right.

HOW SATAN WORKS IN OUR THOUGHT-LIFE

When Adam fell, the human brain was affected. It no longer took its orders from a spirit that was filled with God's Spirit. Being spiritually dead inside, people lived according to what they perceived outside. The biggest outside influence was Satan and his demons. They fed them all kinds of thoughts. Where do you think Cain got the idea to kill his brother Abel? There had never been death or murder in the Garden. Cain didn't know what these things were! Someone had to introduce that idea and image into his mind, and that someone was Satan the destroyer.

When an unbeliever comes to our church, I will be preaching and the devil will tell them, "That man doesn't like you. See how he just looked at you? Do you hear how he's talkin' to you?" That lost soul has no idea that those thoughts are not their thoughts. They have no idea what I really think or feel about them. That's why we take authority over the enemy before we preach and release the Holy Spirit to move in our midst. If an unbeliever comes into our congregation, we want them to hear from God, not the devil. We want them to hear the truth and be set free.

We have seen that our thoughts are not original. Ideas come either from God or the devil. And Jesus taught us that we can take thoughts or not take thoughts. In Matthew 6:31 He said, "Take no thought, saying...." He knows the enemy shoots thoughts at us. As children of God the devil has no access to our spirits but he can introduce thoughts to our minds. We understand from God's Word that we do not have to take any thought the enemy gives us. In fact, if we have a thought that is not saying anything God has ever said in His Word, or we hear something that does not line up with His Word, we need to cast that thing down immediately.

The enemy's job is to deceive people, just like he did Eve. He will use a little of God's Word and then bend it and change it to get us off track and away from God's truth. Then he can trap us in bondage. In Genesis 3:1 he said, "Did God say you couldn't eat of every tree in the Garden?"

Of course, that was not what God said. He said, "You can eat from every tree except one, the tree of knowledge of good and evil. Don't eat of that one or you will die" (see Genesis 2:16-17). The serpent was making God look stingy and controlling, when He was really just warning Adam and Eve of the danger and consequences of eating from that tree. If we go on to read Genesis 3:2-4, we see clearly how knowing God's Word is the only thing that will keep us from deception and calamity.

Unfortunately, Eve didn't understand what God had actually said. She answered the serpent, "Well, God said we shouldn't even touch it or we would die." That's when the snake knew he had her! She didn't know what God *really* said, so Satan went right on to completely contradict Him. The serpent said, "You won't die!" He called God a liar and it went right past Eve.

When Adam came into the picture, he never contradicted the snake. He didn't consult the Lord. He just decided he could do better without Him. He left the authority of God's Word, ate of the forbidden tree, and the rest is history. Mankind's thoughts from that moment on were dominated by Satan and the world system he set up on the Earth.

Jesus gave us the way out of Satan's kingdom and told us we didn't have to take his thoughts. We can reject ungodly images and ideas. If it is a bad thought that contradicts God's Word and gives us a check in our spirits, we should cast it down and meditate on what is true. And if we have a thought that originates outside of us instead of inside of us, we need to compare it to the Word of God. If it isn't of God, we must reject it and go back to meditating on the truth.

If we have a good thought that comes from inside us and lines up with God's Word, we take it. We plant that thought in our hearts, and that idea grows into a new image inside of us. If that new image clashes with an old idea that has been in our lives a long time, we get rid of that old idea that was not godly. We reject it and replace it with God's truth.

This process of renewing or renovating our minds with the Word of God is the opposite of what Adam and Eve did in the Garden. They talked to the serpent instead of God, rejected God's Word, and chose to believe the lies of the devil. But as believers we learn to think right. When a thought comes that runs contrary to the Word or causes uneasiness in our spirits, we kick out the devil and his lies! We stay in communion with the Holy Ghost and line up every thought with the truth of His Word.

CHANGING OUR SET POINT

We have seen how the mind has both a conscious and a subconscious function. Many of our everyday decisions are made by our conscious mind. We see things, evaluate the facts, and choose the best way to go. We are aware of ourselves, our thoughts, the situation, and our decision. But most of us have no idea how many things we say, how many times we react, and how many thought patterns are driven by our subconscious.

The subconscious is that part of us that functions without our conscious perception or the normal mental process. We are not consciously aware of it. If we are asleep and a fly lands on our face, our arm and hand will react automatically to swat that fly off our face. When we wake up, we will have no memory of it because we were not conscious when it happened.

We can also be awake and do things subconsciously. Through the years we have trained ourselves to think, speak, and do things automatically. We have a set point that has been programmed into our subconscious mind. This can be good or bad depending on whether God did the programming or the enemy did the programming. Either way, it's set. It is what we are used to and what we expect.

Renewing our mind includes getting into the subconscious and changing any set point that does not line up with God's Word.

The purpose of the subconscious mind is to keep you from changing, so it rejects change. If you have ridden your bicycle a certain way for twenty years, changing your style is not going to be easy. For a while your conscious mind is going to have to work overtime until the set point in your subconscious mind has been changed. Then one day you will walk out to your garage, grab that bike, get on, and ride it in the new way without consciously thinking about it. You will be halfway down the road before you think, *My, oh my. I'm riding the new way and I didn't even think about it.*

Unfortunately, many of our subconscious set points were programmed by the enemy. When I was a child I experienced some things in my home that weren't too great. As a result, my set points for thought and behavior regarding marriage and family were not based on good role models or teaching.

When I got married, those old memories and patterns began to play. Their job was to make my marriage conform to the set points in my subconscious mind. So about six months into our marriage, I began to get critical of my wife. All I did was find fault. It wasn't long before I was having thoughts like, *Why don't you just leave her? You married the wrong woman. This is not working.*

Now I'm in a dilemma because I'm a Christian, and I know the devil is talking to me about divorce. If my wife had gone out and committed some heinous crime it would be different. But all she was doing was trying to cook me some food! My subconscious mind was trying to make her conform to my set point, which was my mama's cooking! But my wife was not my mama and this was not my father's house. This was our new home, based on the Word of God, and a new set point had to be established. That old set point had to go.

I went to a meeting where a man talked about how confession brings possession. He discussed the power of our words. When we speak, our words go deep into our own hearts and change the way we think. Out of the abundance of our hearts we speak, and what we speak changes the outside. We can reset the inside by speaking, and then we speak from the inside in faith and the outside changes.

I began to confess good things from the Word of God over my wife every day, even though it felt unreasonable to my mind and unsettling in my emotions. I would say, "Oh Lord, I thank You that she's a virtuous woman. She always does me good as long as there's life within her. The bread of idleness, gossip, discontent and self-pity, she does not eat. She gets up early and gets spiritual food for the house. She loves me and admires me exceedingly. Your Word is working in our marriage," and so on.

Every day I confessed this. Every time I had a critical thought I confessed this. I was reprogramming my subconscious mind and changing my set point for my marriage. The set point of criticism established by my past experience was being replaced by the set point of God's vision and purpose for marriage. Spiritual renovation was taking place!

One day I sat down to eat and found myself enjoying everything I ate. I thought, *Man, she is cooking better.* Instead of being critical, I said, "This is gooooood!"

My wife and I began living the high life when I got my mind renewed with God's Word and changed the set points for our marriage to God's set points. We began to prosper in our relationship because our souls were prospering.

> Beloved, I wish above all things that thou mayest prosper and be in health, even as thy soul prospereth.
>
> 3 John 1:2

How does our soul prosper? When our minds are renewed with God's Word and we learn to think right.

FROM EGYPT TO THE PROMISED LAND

From the moment we are born the enemy tries to program our minds, conscious and subconscious, to be like him. He also programs our conscience, which is our moral standard. Our conscience tells us what is right and what is wrong. Therefore, if we are going to think right, we need to get our conscience lined up with God's Word too.

Before I got saved I loved all those worldly songs. Because Satan used to be Lucifer, the archangel who was in charge of praising and worshipping God, he knows the power of music—and he uses it. I used to love to sing that song, "Mrs. Jones...Mrs. Jones...we got a thing goin' on."[1] That song is about adultery! When I got saved I had to stop singing that song and putting that garbage into my heart and mind.

Today we see the horrible results of the devil's music. I wonder how many young men are in prison for murder and rape because of the music they listened to as far back as they can remember. I wonder how many young women are raising kids by themselves on welfare because they were looking for love in all the wrong places and the music they listened to encouraged them to live that way.

Be careful what you listen to! The enemy has structured the world to conform you to evil ways, and one of the biggest snares is music. You say, "But I just like the beat." That beat is enabling that evil lyric to slide right through your conscious mind, pervert your conscience, and program your subconscious mind with a stronghold of wrong thinking. Your heart is being captured by that evil thought, and whatever is in your heart is who you are (see Proverbs 23:7).

When the children of Israel came out of Egypt, they had the same challenges we face today. In the Bible Egypt is a type of the world and the world's system, and Pharaoh is a type of Satan. Israel had spent a lot of years being programmed by the enemy by the time God delivered them. When they got to the Promised Land and the twelve spies came back with their reports, they believed the evil reports because their set point was not based on God's promises. It was based on the wrong thinking of Egypt.

> All the congregation lifted up their voice, and cried; and the people wept that night.
>
> And all the children of Israel murmured against Moses and against Aaron: and the whole congregation said unto them, Would God that we had died in the land of Egypt! or would God we had died in this wilderness!

And wherefore hath the Lord brought us unto this land, to fall by the sword, that our wives and our children should be a prey? were it not better for us to return into Egypt?

Numbers 14:1-3

These people had been slaves in Egypt. Their lives were miserable and oppressed there. Their set point was misery and oppression, so that was all they could see when they heard the good and evil reports about the Promised Land. God had brought them out of Egypt, but Egypt was still in them, so they did not go into the Promised Land. Instead, they wandered in the wilderness for forty years while God tried to get Egypt out of them. He did miracle after miracle to try to replace their old set point of misery and oppression with faith in His Word. Still, their hearts were hard and they resisted God again and again. They chose to continue in their stinkin' thinkin'.

When the people saw that Moses delayed to come down out of the mount, the people gathered themselves together unto Aaron, and said unto him, Up, make us gods, which shall go before us; for as for this Moses, the man that brought us up out of the land of Egypt, we wot not what is become of him.

And Aaron said unto them, Break off the golden earrings, which are in the ears of your wives, of your sons, and of your daughters, and bring them unto me.

And all the people brake off the golden earrings which were in their ears, and brought them unto Aaron.

And he received them at their hand, and fashioned it with a graving tool, after he had made it a molten calf: and they said, These be thy gods, O Israel, which brought thee up out of the land of Egypt.

And when Aaron saw it, he built an altar before it; and Aaron made proclamation, and said, To morrow is a feast to the Lord.

And they rose up early on the morrow, and offered burnt offerings, and brought peace offerings; and the people sat down to eat and to drink, and rose up to play.

Exodus 32:1-6

Moses went up on the mountain to get something good from God, but in their eyes he stayed too long. So now what is coming out of them? What is their automatic reaction to the situation? Egypt started coming out of them. They wanted to build a golden calf like the one the Egyptians worshipped. God was trying to move them out of the ghetto into the nice neighborhood, and all they could think about was how they missed their old gang!

It is never the color of our skin or the fact we came from the other side of the tracks that holds us back. What holds us back from living the high life in Christ Jesus is wrong thinking. When we get to thinking like Jesus, then we will begin to live like Jesus. We will come into prosperity in our families, our churches, our finances, our health, and our callings when our souls prosper.

Think right, and you will live right.

Live right, and every area of your life will prosper.

CHAPTER 6

DON'T FENCE ME IN!

God has always wanted to take His people into the Promised Land. In the Old Testament it was a physical land. In the New Testament our Promised Land consists of the promises of God. Jesus died to redeem us to God and give us abundant life in Him. He died so we could have a relationship with God and obtain everything He promised in His Word. However, most Christians are living below the level of joy and prosperity He wants to give them. The reason for this is that they are more conformed to the world than they are transformed by God's Word.

The world and the enemy are in the business of killing, stealing, and destroying mankind. If they can't keep you from getting saved, then they still will try to keep you from your Promised Land. They will fence you in with lies and deception that make you believe you cannot escape poverty, sickness, depression, a bad temper, sexual immorality, criminal activity, or addictions of all sorts. They will tell you,

"That's the way the men in your family have always been, and that's the way you will be. It's in your blood, man!" Or they'll say, "Women like you can never be happy. Your dreams are unrealistic. Girl, you're livin' in a fantasy world!"

The Bible tells us something entirely different! That is why it is vital that we renew our minds with the Word and keep our minds renewed. Otherwise, we will swallow the devil's lies, be squeezed into the world's mold, and give in to our carnal lusts and patterns of sin. We will continue believing evil reports and miss our Promised Land. We will not live the high life because we have allowed the enemy to fence us into a corner of thinking that there is no way out. We will let him convince us that we cannot overcome, succeed, and be healthy and happy in this life. We will just have to wait until we get to Heaven.

SATAN'S ONLY HOPE: THE BAD SEED

We need to look at this from the enemy's standpoint a minute. Satan's only hope is to stop us from operating in the truth. If he can keep us from abiding in and acting upon God's Word, he can deceive us, he can discourage and frighten us, he can get us entangled in sin and the things of this world, and he can keep us from fulfilling God's call on our lives. In simple terms, if he can keep us from reading, studying, and meditating on the Word day and night, he can steal our divine destiny.

I'm convinced that the reason the church has been very contained, limited, and impotent is because we have not taken seriously the Holy Spirit's admonition to renew our minds and be transformed. Our God is a big God and His plans are big plans. That means we have to learn to think big like He does. When we let the devil fence us in with lies, we shrink God down and His plans become impossible to us. Instead of seeing a Promised Land ripe for the taking, we see giants stomping all over us!

In practical terms, how does the enemy gain control? Because he never had an original thought in his life, he uses God's principles for evil purposes. When Jesus taught the disciples the Parable of the Sower in Mark 4:1-20 He revealed how Satan does this.

> The sower soweth the word.
>
> And these are they by the way side, where the word is sown; but when they have heard, Satan cometh immediately, and taketh away the word that was sown in their hearts.
>
> Mark 4:14-15

Every time we hear the Word, Satan comes to steal it. However, he does not stop at stealing the Word. He also sows his own seeds. Bad seeds! His seeds are designed to lead you away from the truth of God's Word and cause mental blocks. His seed will get you even more entrenched in your ungodly subconscious set points. This bad seed will give the enemy power and influence over your soul, so there will be no way you can prosper in God.

> Beloved, I wish above all things that thou mayest prosper
> and be in health, even as thy soul prospereth.
>
> 3 John 1:2

John related your prosperity to a prospering soul. To root out the bad seed the devil has planted and to be transformed, you must renew your mind with the truth of God's Word. You must sow God's eternal, life-giving seed into your mind and heart—and refuse to let go of it! That is how your soul will prosper and you can rid yourself of the bad seed that has succeeded in fencing you in and getting you stuck in the low life.

WHERE DO YOU STAND?

> My speech and my preaching was not with enticing words
> of man's wisdom, but in demonstration of the Spirit and
> of power:
>
> That your faith should not stand in the wisdom of men, but
> in the power of God.
>
> 1 Corinthians 2:4-5

When Paul says "your faith shall not stand in the wisdom of men," he is saying that your faith will not stand in sense knowledge but in spiritual truth, which is the supernatural power of God. Let me give you an example of what he was talking about. We know that Egypt is a type of the world and Pharaoh is a type of Satan. God brought the children of Israel out of Egypt and out from under Pharaoh's rule to serve and worship Him. When He saves us, He brings us out of the world and out from under Satan's rule to serve and worship Him. We are to stand in Him and His power.

To thrive in the Kingdom of God, we must stand in His power, not ours!

God brought Israel out of Egypt and then took them into the wilderness. He brought them into a place where there was nothing, not even trees for shade! There were no superstores, no convenience stops—not even a soft-drink machine. They had to depend on God to supply everything they needed. In this way He hoped to get the limitations and false perceptions of Egypt out of them and reveal to them who He really was.

What kind of picture does the devil and the world paint of God? What did the serpent tell Eve? "God is keeping you from good things. He doesn't want you to have everything you want. He is judgmental and hard-hearted. You can do much better on your own!" These are the lies that trap people in bondage.

When God wanted the children of Israel to forsake the low life of Egypt and live the high life in His grace and power, He took them into the wilderness to reveal His love and care for them. This was His way of attempting to tear down every fence of doubt and unbelief that was keeping them from receiving His blessings and their Promised Land. He was showing them how much He loved them and cared for them by leading them into a place where they were completely dependant upon Him.

When we are saved and come out of Satan's dark kingdom into the Kingdom of God, we also must depend on God for everything. Then we will come to know Him as He really is. We must deal with the boundaries our previous environment placed in us, those fences that say, "God really doesn't care about you. He doesn't want you to have this. You cannot go there. You are not capable of that. You are not worthy."

These boundaries can show up in so many little situations in life. One of the best examples I witnessed was when I filled up my car with gas one day. After filling the tank I went into the store to pay for it. The attendant asked, "What pump do you have, Sir?"

"Number 9," I answered.

"That will be $36."

The man standing next to me cried out, "$36?!!!"

This guy had nothing to do with me. I didn't know him and he didn't know me. He didn't work at this gas station. But he was extremely shocked that my gas cost $36. Why? Because it was too much for him. The amount of $36 crossed his boundary and ran into his fence!

Satan was using that man to try to get me to come back under those same limitations. The enemy shot a thought at me: *This gas is really going to set me back. I really can't afford it.* But my mind was renewed with God's Word. I knew the truth, and I knew my God. He put His desires in my heart, and it is His will for me to prosper. "I can't afford it" should never be uttered by me! It was His will for me to get that car and drive it, so it was His will for me to fill it with gas. He knew what the economy would be like, and He would provide. So I cast that thought down and smiled. Thirty-six dollars was not a fence in my life because Jesus had set me free!

This is what happens when we are transformed by the renewing of our minds. We no longer stand in the wisdom of Wall Street, popular magazines, or the guy standing next to us at the gas station. We stand in the power of God's Word.

IT'S NOT ALWAYS THE DEVIL

When we renew our minds with God's Word and that renovation process takes place, we can be uncomfortable. It's because we are leaving comfort zones that may have been established when we were children. We got used to those fences, even bad ones. Before we were saved we were comfortable being on welfare and using food stamps. We were comfortable living with our boyfriend or girlfriend and not being married—or being in homosexual or lesbian relationships. We had no problem lying on our income tax forms and using the Lord's name in vain. Then we got saved. We moved into the Kingdom of Light, and the Light began to expose a whole lot of wrong thinking, wrong speaking, and wrong doing.

All of a sudden our "world" became unrecognizable. We found ourselves in this wilderness and all we could do was depend on God and His power to survive. He wanted to bless us beyond our wildest dreams, but we were all bent out of shape at the thought of quitting our job at the strip joint and taking a job at the department store. He wanted to restore our soul, and we couldn't sleep, worrying about how we were going to get along without that homosexual "life partner." And every time we turned around we caught ourselves saying stuff that sounded completely inappropriate and even filthy to our ears.

This wilderness experience can happen to the mature believer too! God wants to deal with some area of our life that needs deliverance or correction, and we blame it on the devil! We will go on and on about how the enemy is messing with us when he isn't messing with us at all. He doesn't have to because he already programmed all that stinkin' thinkin' into us a long time ago. Now God is trying to get it out of us by getting our minds renewed in that area.

The only reason we have the devil's attention now is because he stands to lose the control he has had over us. If we keep renewing our minds with God's Word, he will never be able to touch us again where that issue is concerned. The Word will dynamite those fences, we will smell the sweet fragrance of freedom in the Holy Ghost, and the enemy will be powerless to stop us.

After we are born again the devil is under our feet. He is no longer our primary problem. In the Name and blood of Jesus we have full authority over him and every demon that crosses our path. After we are saved, our primary problem is ourselves! We have been accustomed to thinking in certain ungodly patterns and believing certain unscriptural things, so now we need to make radical changes. And that is not always comfortable. However, if we will trust God and stand in His power, we will be transformed in ways we could not imagine.

IT'S AN INSIDE JOB

My son, attend to my words; incline thine ear unto my sayings.

Let them not depart from thine eyes; keep them in the midst of thine heart.

For they are life unto those that find them, and health to all their flesh.

Keep thy heart with all diligence; for out of it are the issues of life.

Proverbs 4:20-23

In the Hebrew that last verse says that out of our hearts are the "boundaries" of life. The Hebrew word for *issues* can be translated "boundaries."[1] So the boundaries of your life are not on the outside; the boundaries of your life are on the inside of you. And what will change those boundaries so that your life looks more and more like Jesus? You will be transformed by the renewing of your mind with God's Word.

The enemy programmed you to believe that fence is as far as you can go. He told you that is all you can afford. He made you think you were destined to be crippled the rest of your life—crippled mentally, emotionally, and physically. Now God is telling you to kick that fence down, believe Him for that new job, that happy family, that healing, and run like the wind. To do that, you must allow Him to change you on the inside. He wants to renovate your image of Him and what He can do in your life, your image of yourself and who you are in Him, and your perception of the people in your life and the world around you. It's an inside job!

Now that you are a child of God you must remember three things that the enemy wants you to forget. First, your Promised Land was already bought and paid for by the blood of Jesus Christ when you got saved. Everything pertaining to life and godliness was yours the moment you received Him as your Lord and Savior. (See 2 Peter 1:3.) Second, your Father wants you to have it! He wanted you to have it so badly that He gave His only begotten Son to die for your sin so you could be restored to Him and receive it. So don't go around talking about how unworthy you are. You are worthy because God says you are worthy! And third, to possess your Promised Land you must first wrap your mind around it being yours because God wants you to have it. You've got to believe in order to receive it.

The only shortcoming or shortage you have can be found between your ears!

Let's say your soul has been prospering in the Word of God for a time and you find yourself riding in first class on the airplane. Inside you are praising God for all He's done and is doing in your life, and somebody from the old neighborhood walks by on their way to the economy section. They see you, do a double take, and out of their mouth comes, "What are you doin' up here?" You know immediately that your set point has changed and theirs hasn't. Your fences are down and theirs are still in place.

At that moment you have a choice, just like I had a choice at the gas station. You can start to make excuses and go back to talking like you used to talk in the old neighborhood, or you can tell your old acquaintance the truth. "Well, you see, Jesus saved me and I have a brand-new life in Him. He's put me in a high place, a place of peace and joy and success. Do you want Him to save you too?"

Right at that moment you can be either a stumbling block or a sign and wonder to your friend. It all depends on whether or not you decide to stick with God's Word and be transformed or to go back to standing in front of an old fence with an old friend.

It's time for the body of Christ to become the signs and wonders God created them to be in their families, in their old neighborhoods, in their communities, and in this nation. But in order to be a sign and wonder to the people around us, we need to allow God to remove all those fences on the inside of us that are holding us back and replace them with His truth.

WHAT'S REALLY GOING ON WITH YOU?

What happens when you find yourself in the wilderness? You have no food, no water, no shade from the sun during the day, no heat during the cold nights, and no hospital to go to when you get sick. It's just you and God. He takes you into these impossible places to show you two things: who He is and who you are. It's in the wilderness that you find out what He's made of, what He thinks about you, and what He wants to do with you. You also find out what you're made of, what you believe about Him, and what dreams and desires are from Him.

You look into the mirror of God's Word a lot in the desert because there's nowhere else to look! You begin to see where your thinking needs to change and why you've been missing God's best. You find out that the real you is hidden in God in Christ Jesus. The real you is not your physical body, what you are called to do, or how you feel about things. The real you is all wrapped up in Jesus. And the last time I checked my Bible, nothing was impossible to those who believe God's Word and stand in His power. There are no ungodly fences in Christ Jesus!

> Jesus looking upon them saith, With men it is impossible,
> but not with God: for with God all things are possible.
>
> Mark 10:27

It's time for you to recognize the fences in your life and allow God to remove them with the truth of His Word. He has a great life for you, but you can receive that life only if your mind is expanded to think on the grand scale in which He thinks. If you are in the wilderness, you are in a season of great change! Rejoice that lying fences that have held you back for years are being torn down by the truth of God's Word. You are taking your Promised Land!

CHAPTER 7

KOINONIA

I want to go back to the beginning to take another look at just what went wrong in the Garden of Eden. God created the Earth and made it beautiful and fruitful, and He did all this for us. First, He made a wonderful place for us to live, a place of pure luxury. Then He made us in His image and in His class, and He put in us the desire to know Him and fellowship with Him.

We were designed for intimacy with the Creator of the Universe, but it was more than that. He was our Father who loved us as His children. When He lost us to sin in the Garden, He had already made a plan to get us back. He loved us so much that He gave His Son, Jesus, to die and pay the price for our sins so that we could be born again spiritually and be restored to Him as our Father. If that doesn't make you feel special, then nothing's going to make you feel special!

Life in the Garden was amazing, and life in Jesus Christ is just as amazing. Adam and Eve walked and talked with

God. We can do that too. Their communication was spirit to spirit. Ours is too. Their souls were in complete harmony and submission to their spirits, and their bodies were completely whole because they functioned according to the will of their souls, which were right with God in all respects. We can have all that too!

What I want you to see is that the focal point of their lives in the Garden was fellowship with God. Someone once said that fellowship is a couple of fellows in a ship, but the Greek word is *koinonia*. *Koinonia* is a word that covers a lot of ground in a relationship. It means communion, partnership, and sharing.[1] The Bible uses this word to describe our relationship with God and with each other. *Koinonia* encompasses every-thing from the deepest intimacy to mutual benefit, and it produces great creativity and productivity in our lives.

Koinonia is another description of the high life we were created to live with God.

OUR MISSION

God said, Let us make man in our image, after our like-ness: and let them have dominion over the fish of the sea, and over the fowl of the air, and over the cattle, and over all the earth, and over every creeping thing that creepeth upon the earth....

And God blessed them, and God said unto them, Be fruit-ful, and multiply, and replenish the earth, and subdue it: and have dominion over the fish of the sea, and over the fowl of the air, and over every living thing that moveth upon the earth.

Genesis 1:26,28

God did something else. He gave us a mission. We were here first to love and commune with Him, but we were also to have dominion or rule over the Earth with Him as our spiritual head and authority. He commanded us to govern and steward all the resources of the planet in His name.

> The Lord God took the man, and put him into the garden of Eden to dress it and to keep it.
>
> Genesis 2:15

Our mission was also to dress the Garden and keep the Garden. We were to add to the beauty and fruitfulness of it and to guard it. Now something that needs to be guarded has an enemy. So Adam and Eve should have been on the lookout for whatever might come into the Garden to harm it. The problem was, they had never even conceived of harm. They lived in a perfect world and were perfect themselves.

> Out of the ground the Lord God formed every beast of the field, and every fowl of the air; and brought them unto Adam to see what he would call them: and whatsoever Adam called every living creature, that was the name thereof.
>
> And Adam gave names to all cattle, and to the fowl of the air, and to every beast of the field.
>
> Genesis 2:19-20

Adam named every creature. Fish of the sea, insects, and all the birds and animals. He might have looked at how they walked, how they were built, and what they were created to do in order to do a good job in naming them. But really, how did he come up with all those names? You see, he had never been to or had ever visited a university or had access to the Internet.

Adam was able to name all the creatures of the Earth because he was *koinonia* with the Creator. He was one with the Father, the Son, and the Holy Spirit. He did not have to learn anything; he just had to discern the truth from God. Communion, partnership, and sharing with the Trinity was how Adam named those creatures.

The purity, the luxury, the power, and the glory—all honor and blessing—were ours as long as we walked in *koinonia* with our Creator and Father. The success of our mission and the quality and eternity of our lives depended completely upon our fellowship with Him.

THE TEST

We were made in the same class as God so we could live the high life with Him. He wanted family. However, being in His class meant we also had free will. God is not a computerized robot and neither are we. He created humans who could choose to love and serve Him—or not. Adam and Eve were no exception, so He provided a test for their hearts.

> The Lord God commanded the man, saying, Of every tree of the garden thou mayest freely eat:
>
> But of the tree of the knowledge of good and evil, thou shalt not eat of it: for in the day that thou eatest thereof thou shalt surely die.
>
> Genesis 2:16-17

There's the test. God gave them everything except one tree, and He warned them about that tree. If they ate its fruit they would first die spiritually, which meant they would be separated from God, who is the author of all life. Then, because they were spiritually separated from God, eventually their physical bodies would die. In the end they would be separated from God for eternity.

> Now the serpent was more subtil than any beast of the field which the Lord God had made. And he said unto the woman, Yea, hath God said, Ye shall not eat of every tree of the garden?
>
> And the woman said unto the serpent, We may eat of the fruit of the trees of the garden:
>
> But of the fruit of the tree which is in the midst of the garden, God hath said, Ye shall not eat of it, neither shall ye touch it, lest ye die.
>
> And the serpent said unto the woman, Ye shall not surely die.
>
> Genesis 3:1-4

Eve talked to the serpent, and the serpent was controlled by Satan. This is the enemy God had warned them about when He told them to keep and guard the Garden. We can see how Satan operates. He doesn't attack as himself. He attacks through someone or something else, like he used the serpent. We think we are in strife and contention with our relatives, our friends, or our boss; when really we are contending with the enemy who is using them.

The serpent said unto the woman, Ye shall not surely die:

> For God doth know that in the day ye eat thereof, then your eyes shall be opened, and ye shall be as gods, knowing good and evil.
>
> Genesis 3:4-5

The truth was, they were already gods. They were not El Shaddai himself, but they were the children of God. They were in God's class of being. Satan also lied about the consequences of eating the tree of the knowledge of good and evil. He contradicted God's Word to them. God had told them they would die.

At this point Eve makes the mistake of choosing to go with what her mind, physical senses, and something outside of her tells her, instead of going to Adam and God to see what they would tell her. She has left the *koinonia* of God and the saints to go forward on her own. She eats of the tree, and then Adam shows up. We don't know how long Adam has been there, but he also makes the mistake of taking the fruit from his wife instead of talking with God. Instead of continuing in *koinonia* with God, he goes his own way alone.

> When the woman saw that the tree was good for food, and that it was pleasant to the eyes, and a tree to be desired to make one wise, she took of the fruit thereof, and did eat, and gave also unto her husband with her; and he did eat.
>
> And the eyes of them both were opened, and they knew that they were naked; and they sewed fig leaves together, and made themselves aprons.
>
> Genesis 3:6-7

Earlier, in Genesis 2:25, it says that Adam and Eve were naked and were not ashamed. What has changed? No *koinonia* with God. They have died spiritually to Him and suddenly know the guilt, condemnation, shame, and all the bondage that goes with being forever separated from eternal life because of sin. They are cut off from His revelation knowledge and understanding. They have only the soulish knowledge and understanding of good and evil.

We clearly see that after the Fall, Adam and Eve cannot govern and keep the Earth in the power of God and in harmony with Him and each other. They must do it by the sweat of their brows while being at odds with one another. Everything they learn and all their decisions in life will come from their physical senses and be processed by minds that have no spiritual connection with God. They have sunk to a very low level of life.

GOD'S ANSWER

> They heard the voice of the Lord God walking in the garden in the cool of the day: and Adam and his wife hid themselves from the presence of the Lord God amongst the trees of the garden.
>
> And the Lord God called unto Adam, and said unto him, Where art thou?
>
> Genesis 3:8-9

God knew where Adam was. He knew what had happened. No doubt His Spirit grieved when He felt Adam and Eve separate from Him spiritually. But He still reached out to them because His love for them was not changed. He had to expel them from the Garden so that they would not eat of the Tree of Life and live forever in their fallen state, but first He told them the consequences of their sin—and the promise of a Redeemer.

Jesus came to Earth to die on the Cross for our sins and to reconnect us spiritually to the Father. He became the link between us and God. He was the one who put us back together again with our Father. He told us God is not mad at us, that He loves us and wants to bless us in every area of our lives. In Jesus Christ we are fully restored to *koinonia* with our Heavenly Father.

As born-again believers and children of the Most High God, we have only one problem: Our minds have been programmed by Satan, the world, and our physical senses. We have been blind.

> In whom the god of this world hath blinded the minds of them which believe not, lest the light of the glorious gospel of Christ, who is the image of God, should shine unto them.
>
> 2 Corinthians 4:4

Now that we are spiritually alive to God, our spiritual eyes are open. We are no longer spiritually blind! But we must renew our minds so that our thinking will reflect the truth our spiritual eyes now see. We must plant the Word of God in our hearts and hold fast to His Word in order to be free.

TAKE IT CAPTIVE OR BE CAPTIVE

When your sins are washed away by the blood of Jesus at the new birth, the devil knows he has no more authority over you. The only way he can control you is by deception. If he can convince you to make decisions that will bring destruction and death into your life, he can still influence you just like before you were born again.

> This I say therefore, and testify in the Lord, that ye henceforth walk not as other Gentiles walk, in the vanity of their mind,
>
> Having the understanding darkened, being alienated from the life of God through the ignorance that is in them, because of the blindness of their heart:
>
> Who being past feeling have given themselves over unto lasciviousness, to work all uncleanness with greediness.
>
> But ye have not so learned Christ;
>
> If so be that ye have heard him, and have been taught by him, as the truth is in Jesus:
>
> That ye put off concerning the former conversation the old man, which is corrupt according to the deceitful lusts;
>
> And be renewed in the spirit of your mind.
>
> Ephesians 4:17-23

As believers we are not to walk in the vanity or emptiness of our minds. We are to walk in communion with the Spirit, being taught by Jesus, having our minds renewed by the truth of God's Word. Our minds and our thinking should reflect the fact that we are disciples of Jesus Christ. Our thinking, then, should be disciplined to come into agreement with the Word of God. Our thoughts are to be *restrained* by God's Word.

In verse 19 the word *lasciviousness* could be translated "absence of restraint, insatiable desire for pleasure...arrogance, insolence referring to words...wantonness, lustfulness, excessive pleasure...debauchery, perversion in general."[2] A lascivious person does whatever they feel like doing regardless of what the Spirit of God and the Word of God say. Unbelievers are naturally lascivious; but believers have no desire to be lascivious and have the ability to overcome it through the blood of Jesus and Word of God. By taking all lascivious thoughts captive, they will not return to the sins and bondage they lived in as unbelievers.

The Word of God is a benevolent, supernatural restraint.

Everything we speak or do originates with a thought, so the beginning of any lascivious speech or behavior is unrestrained thought. We are commanded to take all evil thoughts captive by the Word of God. One of the best ways to take a thought captive is to immediately push it aside and refuse to speak it out. Remember Proverbs 30:32 says, "If thou hast done foolishly in lifting up thyself, or if thou hast thought evil, lay thine hand upon thy mouth." So cover your mouth whenever you have an ungodly thought.

The next step is to think and then speak what God's Word says instead.

> Finally, brethren, whatsoever things are true, whatsoever things are honest, whatsoever things are just, whatsoever things are pure, whatsoever things are lovely, whatsoever things are of good report; if there be any virtue, and if there be any praise, think on these things.
>
> Those things, which ye have both learned, and received, and heard, and seen in me, do: and the God of peace shall be with you.
>
> Philippians 4:8-9

Be ye followers of me, even as I also am of Christ.

1 Corinthians 11:1

In Philippians 4:9 Paul says to do those things we learned, received, heard, and saw in Paul. In 1 Corinthians 11:1 he says to follow him as he followed Christ. Of all the apostles, Paul was known for his clear, concise thinking. He restrained his mind, which kept his life on track with God and His divine destiny. His example of *koinonia* is the one we are to follow if we want to live the high life in God.

Taking thoughts captive—restraining our thinking, our words, and our actions—is hard sometimes. Satan is still trying to get into our Garden! He will shoot a thought at us and it just seems to go right through that shield of faith and pierce our hearts. *You remember how your friend did you wrong. You remember how that felt, what you went through.* Then your relatives come along and say, "I just saw that jerk down at the ballpark acting like he was in charge or something. Every time I see him I think of what he did to you. I don't know how you can live in the same neighborhood as that guy."

Now you feel like a can of worms was let loose in your mind! You are bombarded with ungodly images, and your emotions are going right along with them. This is when you have to have a renewed mind or get one quick! A renewed mind will tell you who you are as a new creature in Christ Jesus. You are in *koinonia* with the Father and Creator of the Universe. You are in communion with the Holy Spirit, who hovered over the Earth and brought it back to life at the Word of God. You are a joint-heir with Jesus, your Lord and King, the Living Word who never leaves you nor forsakes you. You are not alone in this battle!

Whenever Satan attacks us and tries to get us on a lascivious track, we must stop and remember who we are. We are children of the Most High God. We have learned the lesson of Adam and Eve, and we will not make the mistake of trying to think, speak, and act independently of our Father. We will take this thought to Him immediately, cast all that care on Him, lay it at His feet, exchange our weakness for His strength, and tell the devil where to go!

> Submit yourselves therefore to God. Resist the devil, and he will flee from you.
>
> Draw nigh to God, and he will draw nigh to you....
>
> Humble yourselves in the sight of the Lord, and he shall lift you up.
>
> James 4:7-8,10

You will not live in the vanity of your mind or act according to your physical senses like you did before you were saved if you are continuously walking in fellowship with God. Instead, you will act upon revelation of the Word of God according to the leading of the Spirit of God. Then, in His wisdom and strength, you will be able to restrain your thoughts and take every thought captive. You will forgive the unforgiveable and overcome the impossible because you are in communion, in partnership, and share everything—in *koinonia*—with God. Hallelujah!

CHAPTER 8

THE LAW OF MEDITATION

Beloved, I wish above all things that thou mayest prosper and be in health, even as thy soul prospereth.

For I rejoiced greatly, when the brethren came and testified of the truth that is in thee, even as thou walkest in the truth.

I have no greater joy than to hear that my children walk in truth.

3 John 1:2-4

When we live in *koinonia* with God our soul prospers, and our lives are filled with joy and satisfaction. Our minds are renewed with God's Word, and we walk in the truth. As an apostle of the church, John said he had no greater joy than to hear that those under his leadership were walking in truth. That has got to be the heart's cry of every pastor and church leader, and it certainly is mine. I want to see you, every member of my church, and everyone who hears my teaching walk in truth as a result of my ministry. That is the greatest reward any pastor and teacher could ask for.

God's truth has many facets, but when it comes to living successfully and happily on planet Earth, we must live within the safety and provision of His laws. God's laws, both natural and spiritual, are the absolute truths by which His Kingdom functions. Therefore, we should know His laws and live our lives according to them if we want to live productively and peacefully.

THE JUST AND THE UNJUST

Love your enemies...

That ye may be the children of your Father which is in heaven: for he maketh his sun to rise on the evil and on the good, and sendeth rain on the just and on the unjust.

Matthew 5:44-45

Many people have come to understand God's natural laws and work with them. Whether or not they are saved, they have been able to develop and invent wonderful things just by discovering God's laws. For example, mankind has taken the laws of aerodynamics to cause an airplane to fly. They developed the television, the Internet, and other forms of communication and entertainment in the field of electronics. Just the discovery of electricity and the laws governing it have revolutionized our lives.

Human beings have accomplished all this—and still the world is in turmoil. Why? Only knowing Jesus Christ can change the very inward nature of a person from being sinful to righteous. As believers, we take this one step further. Only when Christians live by God's spiritual laws can their outward life reflect their new, godly nature and impact the world around them.

The spiritual law God has given that is the key to every other spiritual law is often called the Law of Meditation. God reveals this law to Joshua just as he is about to lead the children of Israel into the Promised Land.

> This book of the law shall not depart out of thy mouth; but thou shalt meditate therein day and night, that thou mayest observe to do according to all that is written therein: for then thou shalt make thy way prosperous, and then thou shalt have good success.
>
> Joshua 1:8

The way Joshua and the children of Israel were going to possess the Promised Land was by meditating in God's Word day and night. Today we must possess the promises of God by operating in this same law. We are to literally live in the Word of God at all times. Jesus taught us the Law of Meditation.

> If ye abide in me, and my words abide in you, ye shall ask what ye will, and it shall be done unto you.
>
> John 15:7

> Then said Jesus to those Jews which believed on him, If ye continue in my word, then are ye my disciples indeed;
>
> And ye shall know the truth, and the truth shall make you free.
>
> John 8:31-32

Jesus is the Living Word, and when we abide in Him we abide in the Word of God. He and the Word are the same. Jesus is Truth, and meditating in the Word day and night is how we know the truth, are set free, and stay free. This is also how we get our prayers answered. How this works, again, is very simple. When we think the way God thinks and pray according to His will and Word, then we will have whatever we pray. The catch is, we must believe what we are praying.

WE SEE WITH OUR MINDS

Our physical eyes are the gates through which we contact the world around us, but our minds determine what we actually see with them. How our minds think and the knowledge and wisdom contained in our minds determine what we actually perceive. The Law of Meditation shows us that everything we see is in our minds. What we meditate on is going to determine the way we view everything our physical eyes observe.

When the twelve spies went into Canaan, only two of them saw a great land given by God and prepared for them by God. What they saw in their minds gave them the inspiration and ability to possess it. Why? They were meditating in God's Word, His promises, day and night. They were seeing what God saw and thinking God's thoughts; therefore, they were able to do what God said to do.

The other ten spies still had their eyes on themselves, thinking about what they wanted and what they were capable of doing. They were not meditating on God's promise, so they saw only giants and a land too great to possess. This is a perfect example of how a renewed mind can make the difference between success and failure, just as God told Joshua.

The enemy knows how God's laws work, so he perverts them to accomplish his own evil purposes. In 2 Corinthians 4:4 the Bible says that the devil has blinded the *minds* of those who do not believe God's Word. Notice it did not say he blinded their eyes. It said he blinded their *minds*. We don't see with our eyes; we see through them. We actually take pictures with our minds. The mind is the lens that gives focus to the picture we are taking. Our perspective is formed in our minds.

Meditation deals with the internal, subconscious mind. The subconscious is like a gauge. It holds down growth and expansion—it holds back redevelopment. It doesn't want you to stop doing what you are used to doing. Your subconscious sets boundaries—makes decisions whether you want it to or not—without your conscious participation. The landmarks it sets prevent you from going either below or above a certain level—it will reject any change to keep you in the comfort zone. God designed us with a subconscious mind that goes on automatic pilot to keep us alive and functioning automatically

However, meditation changes all that. It provides you with a spiritual experience that causes your subconscious to look into new information. The Word of God will provide you with a spiritual experience and cause your mind to lock into new information. Caleb had a different outlook or revelation from the other ten spies, which enabled him to say, "Let us go up at once and take possession, for we are well able to overcome it" (see Numbers 13:30). Jacob received new information through a dream from God. The dream not only delivered him from years of servitude and financial bondage to Laban, but also caused a transfer of great wealth to come into his hands. (See Genesis 31:10-12.)

The subconscious is affected by repetition and pondering the Word—by reading it slowly, hearing the Word, often in quiet and rest until your subconscious receives new information. It has the power to transform you.

Satan and his demons try to plant all kinds of ungodly images and thoughts in the minds of people so that when they see the truth they will not recognize it or receive it. We must always remember that Satan and demons have no truth in them.

> Ye are of your father the devil, and the lusts of your father ye will do. He was a murderer from the beginning, and abode not in the truth, because there is no truth in him. When he speaketh a lie, he speaketh of his own: for he is a liar, and the father of it.
>
> John 8:44

If our minds are renewed in God's Word, we will take a godly picture and see as God sees. If our minds are not renewed, or if we reject His Word, we can be deceived and blinded by the devil to see what he wants us to see—and the devil is a liar and the father of lies. If we don't keep our minds renewed and continually submit our lives to the Word of God, the enemy can lead us down the path of destruction and even death.

SIMPLE AND CONSISTENT

One of the things the devil will do is try to complicate everything. But everything God does is easy enough for a child to understand and accomplish. Take the law of gravity. It is very simple. Everything is pulled to the Earth's surface because the Earth is spinning on its axis. Children understand very easily that if they are standing on a chair and jump off of it, they will go down to the ground. They will not fly up into the air. They don't need to know the full scientific explanation to accept the truth and live by it, but it is available to them. This is why Jesus said that we must become like children to be born again and live the Christian life.

> Verily I say unto you, Except ye be converted, and become as little children, ye shall not enter into the kingdom of heaven.
>
> Whosoever therefore shall humble himself as this little child, the same is greatest in the kingdom of heaven.
>
> Matthew 18:3-4

Little children believe what their parents tell them, and they are totally dependent on their parents for love, provision, and protection. That is the way we are to be with our Heavenly Father. We are to believe everything He tells us in His Word and rely completely on Him for everything. Life becomes incredibly simple when we do this, and we understand that everything He asks us to do is simple. Whether it is sowing seeds of faith, abiding in His Word, feeding and clothing the poor, forgiving those who hurt us and offend us, or seeking first the Kingdom—all of His commands are simple.

God's laws are not only simple, but also they are consistent. When I say consistent, I mean they work the same way every time, and they will work for everyone. If it is a law, it will work the same for you as it will for me. The law of gravity will work whether you are rich or poor, black or white, male or female, old or young. Whether you are a high school dropout or have a doctorate in economics, if you jump off the observation deck of the Empire State Building you are going down!

The Law of Meditation is no exception. It is simple. Anyone can do it. And it will work the same for everyone. That is why the devil will take this law and deceive people with it. He knows it will bring results. So he gets people meditating on things other than God's Word. The meditation Satan inspires can bring a season of pleasure and even temporary good into their lives, but ultimately they will find themselves in greater bondage than when they started because they are not meditating in God's Word. They are meditating on things that are not of God.

In recent years the church has stayed away from meditation because there have been so many cults based on some type of meditation. The New Age Movement in all its forms offers numerous ways of meditation. From Transcendental Meditation to Yoga Meditation to Silva Mind Control, people's minds are blinded by the enemy to meditate on what he wants them to meditate on. He deceives them in their minds. They believe they are doing something good, but they are following the greatest liar in the universe.

We must remember that the enemy has never had an original thought. Satan has never created anything. The Bible says that all things were created by and for Jesus Christ (see Colossians 1:16). The devil and his demons can take only what Jesus created and pervert it for their purposes. So the enemy has come up with a multitude of ways to get people to meditate on anything but God's Word. Then he can keep their minds blinded, keep them from believing, and keep them under his control.

Unfortunately, the church has seen all these eastern religions and cults become popular in recent years and many believers have decided that meditation is of the devil. They forgot that God gave the Law of Meditation and that it is a key to our ability to possess all that Jesus died to give us— everything from peace within to financial prosperity without. Therefore, we must look at what the Bible has to say about meditation and practice it as God instructs us.

GOD'S WAY OF MEDITATING

> I call to remembrance my song in the night: I commune
> with mine own heart: and my spirit made diligent search....
> I will meditate also of all thy work, and talk of thy doings.
>
> Psalm 77:6,12

In verse 6 the word "commune" could also be translated "meditate."[1] In verse 12 "meditate" means "to murmur (in pleasure or anger); by implication, to ponder:—imagine, meditate, mourn, mutter, roar,...speak, study, talk, utter."[2] Do you see why God told Joshua not to let the Word depart from his *mouth?* Meditation is not just thinking and pondering but also *speaking.* It is not crazy to talk when no one else is around! And if you want to get technical, God is always there, so you are never really alone. In fact, He is the one you are talking with anyway.

> I remember the days of old; I meditate on all thy works; I
> muse on the work of thy hands.
>
> Psalm 143:5

In this verse "muse" is the same Hebrew word translated "commune" in Psalm 77:6 above.[3] Both of these words refer to meditating God's Word. God wants us to think and say His Word over and over, pondering it in our hearts like a cow chews its cud. If you are a city-dweller, let me explain this analogy.

A cow will chew some grass and swallow it, which is like the first time you hear the Word and receive it. Then the cow will regurgitate what it has just swallowed and chew it some more. This releases more nutrients. Likewise, when you continue to muse on Scripture, to speak it out, ponder it, mutter it, and ask the Holy Spirit about it, you are going to continue to get more and more revelation from it.

The cow continues to do this until all the nutrients in the grass are ingested into its system. This is where meditating the Word differs, because there is no end to the revelation we can glean from God and His Word!

Again, it is so simple! We meditate on His Word day and night and we become one with the Living Word. The Word literally transforms us and enables us to be like Jesus and do the works of Jesus. As long as we are meditating on God's Word, we will do well. And we must always keep in mind that if God's Word is not transforming us, then what-ever else we are meditating on is transforming us.

REPETITION

Advertisers know that if you are constantly being told that only Coke will satisfy your thirst, the next time you go into the store and see a bottle of Coke, that is the first thing you'll pick up. They bombard you with television commer-cials, billboards, radio spots, and magazine ads about how refreshing and thirst-quenching a cold glass of Coke is. Even the world knows that the Law of Meditation works, and it is all about repetition. If you watch movies about having sex outside of marriage all the time, it won't be long before you will be thinking about it all the time and then hopping into bed with anyone who comes along—and believe me, the devil will send them along!

We have to become aware of what we are continually seeing, hearing, experiencing, and thinking. Now I know how it is in this world today. You might be watching a good television program, but the commercials come on and confront you with sickness and death and all kinds of drugs you can take to prevent it. Or you will be driving down the road and see a billboard, and the images are nothing but lust. You are waiting for an appointment and pick up a magazine, only to see all kinds of ungodly images. And watching the news can have you depressed in no time!

There is an old saying, "You can't help the birds flying over your head, but you can keep them from building a nest in your hair." When the world and the enemy and your flesh gang up against you, that's when you go to 2 Corinthians 10:5 and remember to cast down every vain imagination that exalts itself against the knowledge of God and begin meditating on all the wonderful works and plans of God in your life, just as Psalm 143:5 says. Use repetition to eradicate anything the devil throws at you!

We don't meditate on the shopping mall, how fat we think we are, or what we are going to do on Friday night. We meditate on the Word of God day and night. Then, when we go to the mall we will know exactly what God wants us to have. We will be able to eat what the Holy Spirit tells us to eat and pass up the stuff we shouldn't eat. And on Friday night we will find ourselves at the right place at the right time because our minds are in complete *koinonia* with God.

THE POWER OF IT!

Just imagine the whole church, every believer, meditating in the Scriptures day and night. We would easily walk in the Spirit and not in the flesh. We would be proving God's good, acceptable, and perfect will for our lives. We would be connected in the body properly, prospering and in health because our souls would be prospering in the Word. And there would be no limit to what we could accomplish for the Kingdom of God.

The title of this book is "Transform Your Thinking, Transform Your Life" because what we are talking about here is the most powerful—yet simple—key to living a joyful and successful Christian life. The more simple the truth, the greater its power. This is God's design. It takes human beings with the help of the devil to make life complicated and mess it up!

Understanding and practicing the Law of Meditation gives you a confidence that says, "This situation is a real challenge, but I know that if I just meditate in the Word and see this problem the way God sees it, then I will know the truth and be free. I will have His wisdom and be able to make a decision to follow the path that is His will. Meditating in God's Word will deal with this the way it should be dealt with. This problem is nothing more than a miracle-in-the-making!"

I'll tell you how powerful this Law of Meditation is. Whatever you think is what you are and what you will become. You are what you think. You are becoming what you are thinking about. Proverbs 23:7 says, "As he thinketh in his heart, so is he."

My wife said it this way, and I know this is God because there is no improving on it, "If we get the truth and stand on it, everything around us that's not true will have to change." Not only does our own life change when we meditate in the Word day and night, but we have an incredibly powerful, positive impact on the world around us!

If you will alter your thoughts to think like God, you will be astonished at the rapid transformation it will effect in your life. Not only will you have an increased sense of well-being inside, but your body will become healthier, your relationships will improve, and your financial matters will just seem to work themselves out as you follow the leading of the Spirit and do things according to God's Word. All this will happen simply because you changed the way you think by practicing God's Law of Meditation.

CHANGING YOUR SITUATION STARTS INSIDE

Once you understand the transforming power of walking in God's Law of Meditation, find a problem or an area where you are struggling and begin meditating on what the

Word says about that problem. Let's say you are believing God to heal you of some physical sickness or disease. You can change the way your body functions by how you think.

> A merry heart doeth good like a medicine: but a broken spirit drieth the bones.
>
> Proverbs 17:22

If you spend your day meditating on all your symptoms, worrying about your future, and having discouraging and depressing thoughts, your body will just become sicker. Worry is meditating the problem instead of the answer from God's Word, and worry (a broken spirit) will break your body down. Your immune system will become weak. Your heart rate will be irregular. And your negative emotions will cause problems with your digestive system. All that anxiety will constrict your blood vessels and cause circulatory problems.

What you think affects your physical body. I gave a perfect example of this when I told the story of what happened to my physical body after repeatedly watching horror movies. My body was in great dis-ease! Therefore, if you want to obtain the healing God has for you, it is vital that you meditate on what His Word has to say about your body.

> He sent his word, and healed them, and delivered them from their destructions.
>
> Psalm 107:20

This verse of Scripture reveals one of the purposes of God's Word. He gave us His Word so that we could be physically strong to do what He's called us to do and have joy in doing it. His Word literally heals us supernaturally as we read it, study it, and meditate it day and night. Hebrews 4:12 says that God's Word is living and active and powerful. The Word of God supernaturally heals our physical bodies!

Here are some other healing scriptures to meditate so you can get the victory over sickness and disease.

Surely he hath borne our griefs, and carried our sorrows: yet we did esteem him stricken, smitten of God, and afflicted.

But he was wounded for our transgressions, he was bruised for our iniquities: the chastisement of our peace was upon him; and with his stripes we are healed.

Isaiah 53:4-5

Bless the Lord, O my soul, and forget not all his benefits:

Who forgiveth all thine iniquities; who healeth all thy diseases.

Psalm 103:2-3

Who his own self bare our sins in his own body on the tree, that we, being dead to sins, should live unto righteousness: by whose stripes ye were healed.

1 Peter 2:24

When you first read these scriptures, you mentally ascent to the fact that they are true, but they are not the very fabric of your life yet. You must study them. Look up the Greek and Hebrew words. Then meditate on them day and night for them to take root in your soul and transform your thinking. You must chew on them and speak them over and over until you become one with them. Because God's Word is life, when you become one with His Word, His life fills your spirit, soul, and body. This is how the Word heals you.

Meditating on the truth enables us to live in the truth and stand on the truth that we are healed. Jesus paid for our healing with the stripes He took on His back. God sent His Word to heal us. There is healing in His Word. And He heals everything, *all diseases.* As we believe this in the core of our being and see ourselves healthy and whole, knowing God wants us well, we will be healed because our inward condition determines our outward condition.

JUST DO IT

Biblical meditation is God's method of getting a vision of the reality of God's Word. Then His Word determines the outcome of our situation. Meditation is a spiritual process that transforms our belief system and thinking patterns to be like God in an accelerated manner. You see, we were all slaves in Egypt (the world), programmed by Pharaoh (the devil). Every child of Adam and Eve were born into spiritual slavery. But then Jesus saved us and delivered us into the Kingdom of God. Now we have to reprogram our minds to think like God thinks so that we can prosper in His kingdom. We have to purge ourselves of the old slave mentality by meditating on the reality of now being a free child of God.

Some of us were programmed to believe, "Black folks are not as smart as white folks." But the Bible says that Jesus is made unto us wisdom (1 Corinthians 1:30) and is no respecter of persons (Acts 10:34). He is our source of wisdom when we are born again, no matter what color or culture we come from. We have to replace that old program with God's truth. Then we will be free to do what He's called us to do and receive all Jesus died to give us.

When we wanted to start the Joseph Business School, God pointed out a team of people to help set it up. I met with them, told them the vision God had given me, and then asked them to pray, meditate on it, and come back to me with a starting date. They came back and said, "We can have the school up and running in about eight or nine months."

I said, "I had a different time frame in mind. I need to have it up and running in two months."

They began to trot out all the reasons or excuses that it couldn't be done in two months, and finally I said, "Okay. Just start. Take the project and begin with the first step." They came into agreement with that and as soon as they moved forward God began to move miraculously with us. They believed they could take that first step, and when they took it, God was with them. Their faith released His power and resources to do His will.

As believers we must believe what God says! We can't lock ourselves into old patterns of thinking that cause us to say, "I can't," and receive all God has for us. "This is hard," you say. "The world and everyone around me don't believe this way. Every time I turn around I am seeing or hearing something that God's Word says is a lie. People will think I'm crazy if I live like this—going around meditating and speaking the Word."

Just do it! And consider this: the people around you may think you are crazy until you get your family in order and your home full of laughter and joy, get your body healed, get your finances in order, and have a peace about you that they begin to covet. Then they are not going to think you are so crazy! They are going to come to you and say, "Hey! What's happened to you? How've you managed to get your life so together?"

You will simply answer, "Jesus saved me, and I just follow His Law of Meditation. It's real simple. Nothing complicated about it."

"No kidding? What's the Law of Meditation?"

"All I do is think about the truths in the Bible day and night. I talk about the Word with God and with other Christians. I ponder it, meditate on it, and pray it. I let it guide me and comfort me in every situation."

"That's all?"

"Yep, that's all."

Practicing the Law of Meditation simply transforms every area of our lives!

If you think you don't have the time, ask the Holy Spirit to show you how to do it. You can meditate on God's Word when you're doing laundry or driving to work. You can meditate on His works and plans when a problem arises or a relationship goes into turmoil. It won't be long before you will wonder how you ever survived without meditating Scripture day and night!

Most important, your level of intimacy with the Father will grow stronger and deeper. Like any other relationship, the more time you spend with Him, the better you will know Him. More and more you will walk in His character and see His power manifest. So the best advice I can give you today is, "Just do it!"

CHAPTER 9

THE IMPORTANCE OF A GOOD SHEPHERD

Renewing your mind with the Word of God transforms you, and that means you undergo radical changes. It's like going from a caterpillar to a butterfly. From one year to the next, you can look back and barely recognize that you are the same person you were a year ago. With each passing year of walking with the Lord and washing your mind with His Word, you find that your understanding of who you are in Him, your faith in Him, and your confidence in doing what He's called you to do—all these things are growing deeper and more powerful in your life.

More and more God's Word reveals His will for you. He wants you to be happy and full of joy. He wants you to prosper and to walk in health. He wants your marriage to be great and all your children to be saved. That is why He exhorts you again and again in His Word to practice the Law of Meditation because renewing your mind with His truth is the key to receiving everything He wants to give you. He is the Good Shepherd and you are His beloved sheep.

RIGHTLY DIVIDING TRUTH

Jesus saith unto him, I am the way, the truth, and the life: no man cometh unto the Father, but by me.

John 14:6

We have talked about the fact that Jesus is the Truth, the Living Word. Jesus epitomizes and is the essence and substance of Truth. When we read, study, and meditate the Word of God, we are literally partaking of Jesus, the Truth, and becoming like Him.

Study to shew thyself approved unto God, a workman that needeth not to be ashamed, rightly dividing the word of truth.

2 Timothy 2:15

This verse tells us that we can take a word of truth and wrongly divide it. The apostle Paul is letting us know there is a right way and a wrong way to study our Bible. We can take the Word of God out of context by just reading a couple of verses, making assumptions, and not reading and study-ing those verses in context of the whole chapter and book. The next thing we know, we have an interpretation of Scripture we've never heard and think we're so smart—which is exactly what the devil is after.

The devil cannot do anything in your life unless he can pull you away from the Word of God or get you to distort it and pervert it. He will lie to you, deceive you, distract you, tempt you, and seduce you to steal the Word from your heart and keep your mind from being renewed. He will introduce all kinds of lies and deception to get you into error in the Word.

From the very beginning of the church his main strategy was to divide us by doctrinal error and conflict, and he does that the same way he did it with Adam and Eve. He told them there was more to life than what God offered. His strategy is the same today as it always has been. He first gets God's leaders all stirred up, looking for "new revelation." He convinces them that the simple truths of God's Word are boring. To be a "true scholar," they should look for something complicated and intellectual. When they start fishing for something new and different, the enemy is right there to accommodate them.

Unfortunately, ministers are often snared by trying to find a revelation or teaching that "no one has ever preached before." I put that last phrase in quotes because there is nothing new! Ministers who seek out new and different messages from the Bible are usually looking to promote themselves. Deep inside they are not interested in God's truth transforming His people. They are interested in becoming well-known and financially successful.

There is nothing new about this problem either. It was just as big a problem in the Old Testament as it has been under the New Covenant.

> Woe be unto the pastors that destroy and scatter the sheep of my pasture! saith the Lord.
>
> Therefore thus saith the Lord God of Israel against the pastors that feed my people; Ye have scattered my flock, and driven them away, and have not visited them: behold, I will visit upon you the evil of your doings, saith the Lord.
>
> Jeremiah 23:1-2

Obviously, pastors in the Old Testament were not feeding their sheep the right food, which caused the sheep to cease fellowship with other saints, and still the pastors did not care about them. But pastors were not the only ones who were not rightly dividing the Word of God. Many prophets were also prophesying the word of the Lord falsely, speaking from their own hearts instead of speaking God's heart and mind. Their false prophecies were causing the people to walk in error instead of the truth of God's Word.

SPIRITUAL BLINDNESS

> I have seen folly in the prophets of Samaria; they prophesied in Baal, and caused my people Israel to err.
>
> I have seen also in the prophets of Jerusalem an horrible thing: they commit adultery, and walk in lies: they strengthen also the hands of evildoers, that none doth return from his wickedness: they are all of them unto me as Sodom, and the inhabitants thereof as Gomorrah.
>
> Therefore thus saith the Lord of hosts concerning the prophets; Behold, I will feed them with wormwood, and make them drink the water of gall: for from the prophets of Jerusalem is profaneness gone forth into all the land.

Thus saith the Lord of hosts, Hearken not unto the words of the prophets that prophesy unto you: they make you vain: they speak a vision of their own heart, and not out of the mouth of the Lord.

Jeremiah 23:13-16

These prophets were speaking lies that the people wanted to hear so they could continue sinning against the Lord. They were also speaking their personal opinions and visions instead of giving the people the word of the Lord. They did not love God or His people. They just wanted to promote themselves and develop a following. They simply wanted to grow a big church, whatever that took.

In verse 15 above, wormwood was an interesting substance. It actually caused hallucinations. So these leaders were literally spreading their own hallucinations and vain imaginations to those they led. They "got into their own heads" instead of rightly dividing God's Word and spiritually coming to the truth. Therefore, they were spiritually blind and their teaching caused their followers to be spiritually blind.

When Jesus came on the scene, the situation was much the same. Many of the Jewish leaders were concerned only with themselves and had no love or care for God or His people. He called them "blind guides" in both Matthew 23:16 and 24. He also called them "blind leaders of the blind."

Then came his disciples, and said unto him, Knowest thou that the Pharisees were offended, after they heard this saying?

> But he answered and said, Every plant, which my heavenly Father hath not planted, shall be rooted up.
>
> Let them alone: they be blind leaders of the blind. And if the blind lead the blind, both shall fall into the ditch.
>
> Matthew 15:12-14

Jesus said, "The ones who should be able to see, who are in the front, are leading others who can't see, and the ones they are leading are counting on them to see. But they can't see, so everyone is headed for destruction and no one knows it." When Jesus said that the leaders were leading the people into a ditch, He was not just talking about a hole by the side of a road. He was talking about eternal damnation! These blind leaders were leading the people straight to hell.

Jesus was referring to spiritual blindness, which comes by not knowing and believing the truth of God's Word. When you don't know or believe God's Word, you cannot receive the Gospel of Jesus Christ. We know that Satan, "the god of this world hath blinded the minds of them which believe not, lest the light of the glorious gospel of Christ, who is the image of God, should shine unto them" (2 Corinthians 4:4). Only God's Word can open your eyes to see that Jesus is Lord and Savior.

We have discussed the fact that we see with our minds, and it is our minds Satan blinds with deception and lies. After we are born again, he works in the same way. We may profess Jesus as Lord and Savior, but if we do not rightly divide the Word of God, the enemy can continue to deceive us and distract us away from the truth just as he did Eve in the Garden. When we do not know what God's Word really says and follow it, we are blind and cannot see where we are, where we are going, or the impact of what we are doing.

We must know, believe, and live in God's rightly divided truth in order to see clearly.

Truth is simply defined by God as His rightly divided Word. Thus, when we meditate on His Word, we want to make sure that we are meditating on truth that has been rightly divided and is not some strange revelation somebody came up with.

TRUTH REVEALS YOUR MOTIVES

The word of God is quick, and powerful, and sharper than any twoedged sword, piercing even to the dividing asunder of soul and spirit, and of the joints and marrow, and is a discerner of the thoughts and intents of the heart.

Hebrews 4:12

The Word of God is powerful and sharp as a two-edged sword. It will pierce through your soul and spirit and reveal what your true motives are in any given situation. Can you see why pastors, teachers, and prophets who are only interested in promoting themselves would not want to submit themselves to the truth of God's Word? If they did, they would have to deal with their evil intentions and motives.

The Pharisees wanted to build their own personal kingdoms. They weren't building the Kingdom of God for God or looking for His King because they wanted to be their own king. When the King of Truth came and stood right in front of them, doing miracles and teaching with God's authority and power, they could not receive Him. His very presence was the light that was exposing the darkness of their hearts. Eventually, they had to kill Him because the people were following Him instead of them. The people preferred Jesus' compassion and truth to their pride and legalism.

The motives of many of the Jewish leaders were never to feed the sheep, to feed God's lambs. Their motives were to build something big for themselves. But Jesus was the Truth and the Living Word. He knew it wasn't about making followers. It was about raising up kings and priests to God. God is about making leaders: leaders of families, leaders of schoolmates, leaders of communities, leaders of businesses and professions, leaders of artistic expression, leaders in every area of life.

> He answered and said, Every plant, which my heavenly Father hath not planted, shall be rooted up.
>
> Matthew 15:13

In case you are worried about the leaders and believers in the church who are false prophets and teachers and wolves in sheeps' clothing, Jesus promised us that our Father would take care of them. He will pull them out by their roots, and hopefully they will repent and get their hearts filled with the truth of God's Word.

In the meantime, we must look to ourselves! We must not judge the leaders who do this or we will become just what they are. We must pray for them, knowing that we can fall prey to the devil's schemes and become self-centered and proud also. If we want to keep our hearts right with God, we must submit ourselves to the scrutiny and mirror of God's Word day and night, and always be diligent to rightly divide His truth.

GETTING IT RIGHT

There are many areas of the Word of God that are in dispute in the body of Christ, but nothing is more controversial than whether or not God wants His people to prosper and be in health even as their souls prosper. Every leader in the church who preaches God's will to bless us and keep us is continuously under fire by other saints as well as the world. That's because the saints that aren't prospering and in health as their souls prosper are jealous, and the world just hates us and wants us to remain poor, sick, and ignorant of the promises of God.

This is not new. Jesus dealt with the same stuff in His time on Earth.

Then the Jews took up stones again to stone him.

Jesus answered them, Many good works have I shewed you from my Father; for which of those works do ye stone me?

The Jews answered him, saying, For a good work we stone thee not; but for blasphemy; and because that thou, being a man, makest thyself God.

Jesus answered them, Is it not written in your law, I said, Ye are gods?

If he called them gods, unto whom the word of God came, and the scripture cannot be broken.

John 10:31-35

Jesus didn't pull a rabbit out of a hat when He said "Ye are gods." He went back to the Old Testament and quoted it. He quoted a verse that every one of the Jewish leaders had read time and time again in their synagogues and in the Temple. But as many folks will do, they only accepted and received what fit into their comfort zone. They took a little bit of this and wouldn't take that. They refused to submit themselves to the whole council of God.

This particular verse, which says that the saints are *gods,* is one of those controversial issues that few preachers and teachers will touch. It is because they have been so programmed to believe what the Word doesn't say that they just can't believe what it does say. The world and certain denominations are caught up in a false humility, which has deceived many saints into having a wrong image of who they are in Christ Jesus.

Too many believers have been taught that God and Jesus are way up in Heaven, and Christians are way down here in this old, dirty world. Saints aren't really saints. They are filthy, unworthy worms in the sight of Almighty God. They are "sinners saved by grace," and what they mean is that the blood of Jesus just barely allows them to slip into Heaven when they die. But that's not what the Bible says.

God, who is rich in mercy, for his great love wherewith he loved us,

Even when we were dead in sins, hath quickened us together with Christ, (by grace ye are saved;)

And hath raised us up together, and made us sit together in heavenly places in Christ Jesus:

That in the ages to come he might shew the exceeding riches of his grace in his kindness toward us through Christ Jesus.

Ephesians 2:4-7

When we were saved, God raised us to sit at His right hand with Jesus. Positionally, we are sitting in Heaven with Him. We are on the same level as God. Jesus also pointed out the fact that in the Old Testament God called us *gods*.

I have said, Ye are gods; and all of you are children of the most High.

Psalm 82:6

God called us gods because we were created in His likeness, in His class. He's not intimidated or scared to call us gods because He knows we aren't ever going to be Him! He's the Most High and we are just high. We are His children and under His authority, living the high life in Him.

The devil programs people to stay away from this truth because it deals with the revelation of who we are in Christ Jesus. He knows this truth will transform our image of who we are in relationship to our God and Father. And when we get it right, the enemy loses most of his ability to deceive us and tempt us. Knowing the truth makes us free! We can sit in Heaven, speak our Father's Word and will into the Earth, and all His power is released to perform that Word.

When you know and rightly divide the truth that you are a little god under the Most High God, you no longer need a false humility because you are so humbled that He would raise you up, seat you with Him as His child and joint-heir with Jesus, and give you the authority and power of His name. That is real humility! And with that truth and humility you can take back every dime the devil's stolen from you and more. When the greatest physicians and hospitals say, "I'm sorry, nothing can be done for them," you can say, "Let me pray the prayer of faith and they shall recover." You can solve every problem in your marriage and in your children's lives. And you can lead people to the Lord and get them free too!

Your problem is no longer lack of education or money, the neighborhood you come from, your skin color, your personality, or your boss. Now your only problem is a lack of truth, ignorance of *what God's Word really says* about you, the situation you are facing, and the world around you. Your problem is simple ignorance of the truth that will make you free. And you can get the truth you need by rightly dividing the Word of God, believing it, and living it.

SEEING FROM GOD'S PERSPECTIVE

God has raised us up to sit with Jesus in Heaven, but we are not just to sit. He has stuff for us to do. Let's go back to Psalm 82 and read that whole passage on us being *gods*.

God standeth in the congregation of the mighty; he judgeth among the gods.

How long will ye judge unjustly, and accept the persons of the wicked? Selah.

Defend the poor and fatherless: do justice to the afflicted and needy.

Deliver the poor and needy: rid them out of the hand of the wicked.

They know not, neither will they understand; they walk on in darkness: all the foundations of the earth are out of course.

I have said, Ye are gods; and all of you are children of the most High.

Psalm 82:1-6

Being conformed to the image of Jesus Christ also means doing the works of Jesus. Our Father is sitting up there saying, "How long are you going to just sit and watch all this wickedness in movies, on television, and over the Internet? What are you going to do about these young kids shooting each other? What are you doing about the poor and the sick? How long has it been since you shared the Gospel with someone? There are people all around you who are dying and going to hell, and you're just walking by them."

God has a right to ask us that because He created us as gods and gave us dominion over this Earth. We are the rulers of this entire planet! This planet was made to obey the sons and daughters of the Most High.

Ye are blessed of the Lord which made heaven and earth.
The heaven, even the heavens, are the Lord's: but the earth hath he given to the children of men.

Psalm 115:15-16

The enemy does not want the shepherds to be telling the sheep this because then we might not only get transformed ourselves but also transform this planet into the Kingdom of God. Satan would be completely locked out!

If we don't know who we are, we are subject to act like anybody. On the other hand, if we understand who we are in Christ Jesus, then we are going to act like Jesus. That is what the devil is afraid of, and it is what all of creation is crying out to see!

Before I was saved, when I was a little boy, I thought I was Superman, donning my cape and saving the world. Then I was The Lone Ranger, running around the house with a mask on. Next I was Tonto because I felt the Indians had been rejected. Later on, listening to popular music, I thought I'd like to be James Brown, singing, "I feel good!" I had no idea who I really was. I was being molded by the world in which I lived.

Then I got saved, praise God! It took some time of renewing my mind, rightly dividing the Word of God, but I'm really getting ahold of the fact that the enemy is under my feet (Luke 10:19) because I'm a joint-heir with Jesus Christ (Romans 8:17). And I thank God for the pastors and teachers who have helped me and continue to help me understand who I really am in Christ Jesus.

Good shepherds tell us who we are in Jesus and teach the whole counsel of God. They don't have soap boxes and petty doctrines to build themselves a following. They want to see the body of Christ transformed. We are little gods who are children of a big God, the one and only true God. When we rightly divide the Word of God, we can see this and God can raise up a people who will reach the world for Jesus Christ. The key is to let Him raise us up! Galatians says it all.

Now I say, That the heir, as long as he is a child, differeth nothing from a servant, though he be Lord of all;

But is under tutors and governors until the time appointed of the father.

Even so we, when we were children, were in bondage under the elements of the world:

But when the fulness of the time was come, God sent forth his Son, made of a woman, made under the law,

To redeem them that were under the law, that we might receive the adoption of sons.

And because ye are sons, God hath sent forth the Spirit of his Son into your hearts, crying, Abba, Father.

Wherefore thou art no more a servant, but a son; and if a son, then an heir of God through Christ.

Howbeit then, when ye knew not God, ye did service unto them which by nature are no gods.

But now, after that ye have known God, or rather are known of God, how turn ye again to the weak and beggarly elements, whereunto ye desire again to be in bondage?

Galatians 4:1-9

In verse 8 the Bible says that before you were born again you "did service unto them which by nature are no gods." You served a world of unbelievers and demons who were not gods. Then in verse 9 it says, "But now...!!!" You are not a servant; you are a son or daughter of the living God. So why do you continue to live like you are a weak nobody in bondage?

Who we are in Christ Jesus is just one of the many issues that can get distorted and perverted by teachers who don't rightly divide God's Word and teach the whole counsel of God. They don't study, look up the Greek and Hebrew, ask the Holy Spirit to lead them and guide them, and read it and meditate it in context. They don't consider who is speaking and to whom. They don't consult all the great commentaries and references we have available today. And, most important, they are too proud to talk with someone more mature than they are about the parts they just can't seem to understand. Instead, they make the Bible say what they want it to say or what they have been trained to believe it says. Either way, they cause trouble in the church.

When you meditate God's Word, study it first. Put yourself under the guidance and leadership of a pastor and listen to teachers who are good shepherds. You want to hear those who teach the whole counsel of God and not just their favorite parts, who will tell you the truth, the whole truth, and nothing but the truth!

CHAPTER 10

HOW LONG ARE YOU SLACK?

Now after the death of Moses the servant of the Lord it came to pass, that the Lord spake unto Joshua the son of Nun, Moses' minister, saying,

Moses my servant is dead; now therefore arise, go over this Jordan, thou, and all this people, unto the land which I do give to them, even to the children of Israel.

Every place that the sole of your foot shall tread upon, that have I given unto you, as I said unto Moses.

From the wilderness and this Lebanon even unto the great river, the river Euphrates, all the land of the Hittites, and unto the great sea toward the going down of the sun, shall be your coast.

Joshua 1:1-4

These verses begin the account of Joshua stepping into the ministry of Moses, getting ready to lead the children of Israel into the Promised Land. This was a pretty tall order because Moses had delivered them from slavery in Egypt, parted the Red Sea, got water out of a rock, and had manna rain down every morning. All this happened because he was the one who communicated with God. However, God promised He would be with Joshua just as He had been with Moses.

> There shall not any man be able to stand before thee all the days of thy life: as I was with Moses, so I will be with thee: I will not fail thee, nor forsake thee.
>
> Be strong and of a good courage: for unto this people shalt thou divide for an inheritance the land, which I sware unto their fathers to give them.
>
> Joshua 1:5-6

God also gave Joshua the key to strength, courage, and success: the Law of Meditation. He gave all of us a systematic way to renew our minds and see our lives transformed. Then we will not be conformed to this world but instead be transformed by God's Word (Romans 12:2). And the reason God wants our minds to be renewed is so He can use us to do mighty exploits in this Earth. We are all Joshuas, and each of us has a Promised Land to conquer and enjoy with the Lord.

> Only be thou strong and very courageous, that thou mayest observe to do according to all the law, which Moses my servant commanded thee: turn not from it to the right hand or to the left, that thou mayest prosper whithersoever thou goest.
>
> This book of the law shall not depart out of thy mouth; but thou shalt meditate therein day and night, that thou mayest observe to do according to all that is written

therein: for then thou shalt make thy way prosperous, and then thou shalt have good success.

Joshua 1:7-8

I want you to understand that meditating God's Word is not a passive, wimpy thing. Meditating God's Word meant winning battles to Joshua, and it means winning battles to you! You are taking the land God has given you. And that process begins by changing the way you think about God, yourself, and every issue in your life. You literally wage spiritual war over the strongholds that have been programmed into your mind by the enemy, strongholds of thought that have held you back and kept you in bondage.

Meditation is the means by which we envision God's Word coming to pass in our lives. We take His truth like a sword and actually destroy our old, ungodly self-image and build a biblical one. We renovate our brains! We expel the devil's lies and falsehoods by building new thought patterns of truth. We no longer see ourselves as weak and stupid and ugly! The joy of the Lord is our strength (Nehemiah 8:10), Jesus is our wisdom (1 Corinthians 1:30), and we are His beloved (2 Thessalonians 2:13).

Biblical meditation is a spiritual experience in which we supernaturally become more and more like Jesus, and that demands action.

PUTTING ON THE NEW MAN

We have talked about how meditation transforms the conscious and subconscious parts of our minds and also our conscience. The conscience is where our moral standards are set, but the Bible says that it can be seared or become dull by habitual sin, ungodly traditions, and the world's reasoning. The enemy tries to program our conscience to be open to anything, especially evil and wicked practices.

> Now the Spirit speaketh expressly, that in the latter times some shall depart from the faith, giving heed to seducing spirits, and doctrines of devils;
>
> Speaking lies in hypocrisy; having their conscience seared with a hot iron.
>
> 1 Timothy 4:1-2

When our conscience becomes seared we have no problem lying and believing our own lies. But when we begin meditating in God's Word, the darkness of deception is exposed by the light of God's truth. We then begin the process of putting off the old man and putting on the new man.

We cannot put the new man on top of the old man, or eventually the old man will emerge and take over again. We want our soul to reflect the reality of our new birth. We are brand new in our spirit, and now our soul must put off the old man of sin and put on the new man of righteousness, which is who we really are in Christ Jesus.

> That ye put off concerning the former conversation the old man, which is corrupt according to the deceitful lusts;
>
> And be renewed in the spirit of your mind;
>
> And that ye put on the new man, which after God is created in righteousness and true holiness.
>
> Ephesians 4:22-24

God wants a total renovation in your thinking. He wants all the old lies and corruption and perversion thrown out and replaced by His powerful, simple truth. It is only as you learn to think, speak, and act like God that He can use you to reach this world with the integrity and compassion of Jesus. Putting on the new man is not passive. It is aggressively pursuing who you are and what you have in Christ Jesus.

STORMING THE GATES OF HELL

I find so many Christians are passively sitting, waiting on God to do something, when God has already done everything! He did it through the life, death, and resurrection of the Lord Jesus Christ. Through Jesus we have been restored to God as His children, we are righteous and have no desire to sin anymore, in His name and through His blood we have authority over the enemy, and we have no reason to fear anyone or anything. We have His peace, His wisdom, and His power. When His Word comes out of our mouths in faith and according to His will, what we speak must come to pass. So what are we waiting for?

Even when we are not moving forward physically, we must always move forward mentally. It is vital that we continue to take the land of our minds by meditating in God's Word day and night. We must eat, sleep, and breathe truth. This is not a passive thing! This is literally storming the gates of hell.

God really wants Christians to be on the offensive, pushing back and conquering every device and system of the enemy. Jesus said the gates of hell would not prevail against us (Matthew 16:18), but if we are not moving forward they are pushing us back! We must put feet to our faith, take dominion, and make disciples of all nations. We must be the Kingdom of God in this Earth and bring Heaven to Earth, just as He originally intended us to be and to do.

Yes, we have giants to overcome, just like Joshua and the children of Israel. And how did they overcome those giants? By meditating in God's Word day and night until they no longer saw themselves as grasshoppers but as conquerors. They no longer saw the Promised Land as the enemy's territory. The Promised Land was theirs! This was their land and God wanted them to have it, so He would show them how and give them the strength to possess it. All of this was possible only because they meditated on the Word and changed the way they thought.

The children of Israel were called by God to occupy the land He had given them, and each of us is called to occupy the land He has given us. In Luke 19:12, Jesus told the story of a nobleman (who was a type of Jesus) who commanded his servants to occupy his land until he returned. After His resurrection and just before He ascended to the Father in Heaven, Jesus gave this command to the church.

> He said unto them, Go ye into all the world, and preach the gospel to every creature.

He that believeth and is baptized shall be saved; but he that believeth not shall be damned.

And these signs shall follow them that believe; In my name shall they cast out devils; they shall speak with new tongues;

They shall take up serpents; and if they drink any deadly thing, it shall not hurt them; they shall lay hands on the sick, and they shall recover.

So then after the Lord had spoken unto them, he was received up into heaven, and sat on the right hand of God.

And they went forth, and preached every where, the Lord working with them, and confirming the word with signs following. Amen.

Mark 16:15-20

Obviously Jesus had a vision of a church that was aggressive, powerful, and compassionate in their faith. And from verse 20 it looks like the early church received and embraced that vision. There is nothing passive about the Great Commission!

POSSESS WHAT GOD HAS ALREADY GIVEN

Joshua put what I am saying into words when he dealt with seven of the tribes of Israel who had not taken their land yet. Even after the enemy had been defeated, some of the people were not moving forward to possess what God had already given them.

The whole congregation of the children of Israel assembled together at Shiloh, and set up the tabernacle of the congregation there. And the land was subdued before them.

And there remained among the children of Israel seven tribes, which had not yet received their inheritance.

And Joshua said unto the children of Israel, How long are ye slack to go to possess the land, which the Lord God of your fathers hath given you?

Joshua 18:1-3

I looked up the word "slack," and it is the Hebrew word *raphah*. *Raphah* means "to be slack, be remiss, be idle...to be weak, be feeble; to desist...to sink down, to be despondent, be disheartened; to be lazy...to loosen...let fail, let drop; to withdraw...to let alone, abandon, desert...to leave off, quit....The basic idea of relaxing the hands, a letting down, can connote the loss of courage."[1] Being slack is the opposite of what God said Joshua would become from meditating the Word day and night: strong and of a good courage.

The question I'm asking you right now is, Are you slack in your walk with the Lord?

I will preach something on Sunday morning and the people cry, "Amen, Pastor, that's good! I got this!" Then by Monday afternoon they stand around the break room with their co-workers and get talked out of everything they heard the day before. They turn on the news and get discouraged. Their family has a crisis and they lose hope. All their faith seems to disappear in the busyness, problems, and distraction of daily life.

How does this happen? They are slack. They forgot that they are called and equipped by God to storm the gates of hell and possess everything Jesus died to give them—and that begins in their thought life.

Our hearts sink because our thoughts stink!

We have to stop being so easily persuaded away from what God's Word says about us and what we have in Christ Jesus. We have to be strong and of a good courage, moving forward in faith to take possession of what God wants us to possess. He wants us to possess the Earth! He commanded us to make disciples of all nations, to lead the lost to Jesus and teach them His Word. The harvest is out there, and if we don't bring it in according to God's timing, it will rot in the field.

DEALING WITH UNBELIEF

It should be obvious to us by now that if we don't think we can do it, we won't do it. It's just that simple. This is where biblical meditation comes in. As we meditate in God's Word day and night, we will be strong and of a good courage. We will not be slack because meditation in the Word of God enables us to see that all things are possible to those who believe.

In the Gospel of Mark, Jesus was approached by a man whose son was possessed by an evil spirit. The disciples had tried and failed to cast the demon out of him.

He answereth him, and saith, O faithless generation, how long shall I be with you? how long shall I suffer you? bring him unto me.

And they brought him unto him: and when he saw him, straightway the spirit tare him; and he fell on the ground, and wallowed foaming.

And he asked his father, How long is it ago since this came unto him? And he said, Of a child.

And ofttimes it hath cast him into the fire, and into the waters, to destroy him: but if thou canst do any thing, have compassion on us, and help us.

Jesus said unto him, If thou canst believe, all things are possible to him that believeth.

And straightway the father of the child cried out, and said with tears, Lord, I believe; help thou mine unbelief.

Mark 9:19-24

We do not want to be a faithless generation! All things are possible to us if we have faith, if we believe God and His Word. Unfortunately, many of us are slack because of unbelief. Unbelief is not nonbelief. Nonbelief is believing nothing. Unbelief is not believing God's Word. We are called believers because we believed on the Lord Jesus Christ as our Savior, gave Him our lives, and believe and live in His Word. Unbelievers do not believe in Him or His Word. Unbelief is a hostility and skepticism toward God, a rejection of His true nature and the absolute truth of His Word.

The problem is, when we get saved our minds don't believe a lot of things God says in His Word because we have been programmed not to believe those things. The Bible says we are healed physically, but the television commercials continue to tell us that we need all kinds of medications to keep us healthy. Flu season is here and everyone around us has got it or is getting a shot for it. We need to turn off the TV and open our Bibles!

The devil is trying to get us to think and believe what we thought and believed before we got saved, before we started reading, studying, and meditating God's Word. Remember, he knows that we are what we think! He knows that if we turn off that TV and meditate God's Word we will think like God and walk in health. The quality of our Christian lives depends on the way we think.

We defeat and eradicate unbelief from our souls by not being slack in meditating God's Word and moving forward in faith.

As a Man Thinketh

There was a crippled man who went to a tent crusade and heard the Word of God concerning healing. He believed, and when the man of God laid hands on him he got healed. After he went home, for several days he was just fine. Then one day his old pastor came to visit. They talked about old times for a while, and then the subject turned to healing. The pastor said, "You know, God doesn't heal everyone."

That statement of unbelief was like a fiery dart of the enemy, and the man didn't know enough to quench that dart with his shield of faith and choose to believe God's Word over what his pastor was telling him. That fiery dart took hold of that man's thoughts and captured his heart.

When the pastor got up to leave, the man could not move his legs. His old malady had come back because he had been slack. He had not continued believing and moving forward in faith. He stopped, he doubted what God had said, he became disheartened, and he was persuaded not to believe. He lost his healing, because as a man thinketh, so is he. He was in unbelief.

Don't minimize the power of your thoughts! What you think controls your body and determines your destiny. I went to see a relative of mine who had just gotten out of the hospital. They said to me, "You know, you're going to have this too." Fortunately, my mind was so renewed concerning the truth about healing and being free of all generational curses, I just looked at them and said, "No, I'm not going to have that." But if I had been slack about being transformed by the Word of God and persevering in it, I probably would have developed the same problem my relative had.

> A good man out of the good treasure of his heart bringeth forth that which is good; and an evil man out of the evil treasure of his heart bringeth forth that which is evil: for of the abundance of the heart his mouth speaketh.
>
> Luke 6:45

I spoke what was in my heart, what I thought and believed, and I have never had that problem, praise God!

> Keep thy heart with all diligence; for out of it are the issues of life.
>
> Proverbs 4:23

Remember, the word "issues" could also be translated "boundaries" or "borders."[2] Out of your heart come the boundaries and borders of your life. What's stopping you is not on the outside; it's on the inside! You are what you think you are. You can do what you think you can do. You will go as far as you believe you can go. Therefore, God can use you only to the degree to which you believe His Word.

The story is told about John G. Lake, that when he was in Africa the bubonic plague struck his area. Many were dying, and Lake refused to take all the precautions the medical community suggested. When asked why, Lake declared the plague would not hurt him. To prove his point, he asked the doctor to put some infected saliva on a slide from a man who was sick with the plague. They looked at it through the microscope and saw the microbes of the disease running around.

Next Lake took the slide from underneath the microscope and wiped the saliva from it on his hand. The doctor was aghast, but Lake calmly took another slide and wiped the saliva from his hand on it. Then the doctor looked at it under the microscope. The microbes were dead!

The doctor asked, "What's your secret?" Lake replied that he meditated on Psalm 91 and other scriptures of protection and provision from the Word of God. Lake believed what God said. By the stripes of Jesus he was healed (1 Peter 2:24), no plague would come hear his house (Psalm 91:10), and nothing could hurt him (Luke 10:19).

If John G. Lake had been slack, he would not have lived through that plague and fulfilled what God had him to do in Africa. The impact he had is still felt today. His ministry was one of the first ministries to have church meetings with both blacks and whites present! This was a very dangerous situation, but God could use him because his faith was steadfast.

Don't be slack. Be on the offensive in faith. Meditate in God's Word day and night, believe what He says, and possess everything He has for you! And don't let anyone talk you out of believing. Whether it is winning a thousand souls to the Lord next year, getting a scholarship to college, or buying your first home, believe and receive what God has already given you.

Furthermore, when you come across someone who believes more and thus possesses more than you, don't put them down, resent them, or get jealous! Let their faith challenge you to go deeper into God's Word and reject the boundaries and borders the enemy has placed on your mind. Decide today that you will only think the way God thinks, and all things will be possible to you.

GET INTO
THE IMPOSSIBLE

For verily I say unto you, If ye have faith as a grain of mustard seed, ye shall say unto this mountain, Remove hence to yonder place; and it shall remove; and nothing shall be impossible unto you.

Matthew 17:20

Jesus said unto him, If thou canst believe, all things are possible to him that believeth.

Mark 9:23

Jesus beheld them, and said unto them, With men this is impossible; but with God all things are possible.

Matthew 19:26

Jesus really got fired up about His disciples getting into the impossible with God, and if He wanted them to move in the realm of the impossible, He wants us to move in the realm of the impossible too. What is the impossible? It is anything that is not possible in the natural or physical world we live in. That which is impossible is that which we know natural laws forbid, our minds cannot reason out, or our physical senses cannot perceive.

Sometimes God gives us discoveries of other natural laws that override the natural laws we knew, and that makes something possible that was not possible before. For example, for a long time we thought human beings could not fly. Then the Wright Brothers discovered the laws of aerodynamics. They found that the laws of aerodynamics would override the law of gravity so that an airplane could fly. Mankind got into the impossible and flew by working with laws of nature they didn't know existed before.

Some people would say that flying is a miracle, but we were just discovering more of God's natural laws. Jesus was talking about getting into the spiritual realm of possibility that overrides all natural laws. We get into the impossible when we believe God and His Word with every fiber of our being. What we believe may seem illogical and impossible to human thinking, but it is no challenge to the Creator of the Universe—who just happens to be our Daddy!

NOT OF THIS WORLD

When we declare what the Word of God says and a person comes up to us and says, "That's impossible," their standard is natural law and worldly reasoning. They have been programmed by the enemy to believe they cannot move beyond natural boundaries and limitations. Being children of the Most High God, however, we are in this world but not of this world. Heaven is our home and Earth is where we are ambassadors for Christ (2 Corinthians 5:20). Our standard is Heaven not this fallen world.

> Thy kingdom come. Thy will be done in earth, as it is in heaven.
>
> Matthew 6:10

We are citizens of the Kingdom of God, dwelling in a place where everything happens by faith in God and His Word. And, as Jesus said, if we can believe, all things are possible to us. A whole new world opened up to us at the new birth. The Kingdom of God operates on believing. What is impossible to the natural man and woman is possible to the spiritual man and woman who believe God and His Word. That is why God told Joshua to meditate in the Word day and night. He wanted the children of Israel to change their thinking and get into the impossible.

ABIDE IN THE WORD AND WALK IN THE SPIRIT

Boundaries and limitations only occur in believers' lives when they do not believe God and His Word. To expand our capacity to believe, then, we read, study, and meditate on His Word day and night. We commune with our Teacher, the Holy Spirit, and we act according to His leading. Abiding in the Word and following the Spirit get us into the impossible. We begin to see and believe things we never could see and believe before.

> If ye abide in me, and my words abide in you, ye shall ask what ye will, and it shall be done unto you.
>
> John 15:7

> There is therefore now no condemnation to them which are in Christ Jesus, who walk not after the flesh, but after the Spirit.
>
> For the law of the Spirit of life in Christ Jesus hath made me free from the law of sin and death.
>
> Romans 8:1-2

The fallen world operates according to the law of sin and death, but the Kingdom of God operates according to the Spirit of life in Christ Jesus—abundant life. I'm talking about a life that has unlimited potential and possibilities for growth, blessing, and success. We have been freed from the constrictions, oppression, and limitations of sin and death. Now we can walk as Adam and Eve once walked with God in the Garden!

THE PURPOSE OF PRESSURE

The inheritance God has for us in Christ Jesus is beyond our natural ability to conceive or obtain. It's too big for our bank accounts, is way beyond our education, and completely outruns our physical strength. We find this out when we get under pressure. God tells us to do something impossible, and in faith we take the first few steps, then the pressure comes. This reveals just what we believe and don't believe when it comes to the Word of God. If we get into God's Word and allow the Holy Spirit to change our thinking, we will get into the impossible and move forward. I have learned this again and again!

In the fall of 1997 we formed Forest Park Plaza, Inc., to acquire a mall and to create a strong partnership with village officials, retailers, and local residents. Our goal was to be a place where the integrity of God was the foundation for success and to enhance the economic life of the people in our community. When we were building the mall, all construction stopped suddenly when funds ran out. I went to the bank to obtain a loan to continue the work, but during that time it looked like the project had been deserted.

To anyone passing by the mall, it seemed like nothing was happening—and everybody was looking at me. It was a very embarrassing predicament to be in! Somebody came to my office and read Luke 14:28 to me, which essentially says, "What man goes out to build a building without first counting the cost? If he doesn't count the cost, he'll find himself being embarrassed when he doesn't have enough money to build it." The pressure was really on me!

Instead of getting all offended, I got back in the Word and stayed there until my ability to believe was up to the challenge in front of me. I read in Joshua 1:3 that God had given me every place the sole of my foot tread upon, and I had surely tread upon the land where the mall was! I reviewed all God had said to me when He gave me the vision for the mall and confirmed that it was His will to build it. I prayed in the Spirit and built up my faith. It wasn't long before we were moving forward again, and my capacity to believe was bigger and stronger than before.

Meditating God's Word turns pressure into prosperity.

LABAN'S LESSON

The Bible gives us many great examples of how abiding in God's Word can turn the pressures of life to our advantage. One of them is found in chapters 29 and 30 of Genesis, where we see how Jacob handled his father-in-law, Laban.

Laban had two daughters, Leah and Rachel, and Jacob wanted to marry Rachel. So Laban told Jacob that he could marry Rachel in exchange for seven years of labor. Jacob agreed and worked the seven years, but the morning after his wedding night he discovered that Laban had given him the homely Leah not beautiful Rachel. Furious, Jacob went to Laban to demand justice. Laban said that Jacob could have Rachel only if he worked another seven years for her. Jacob agreed.

Now Laban didn't just want a free worker to help around the farm. He didn't just want to unload the oldest, not-as-good-looking daughter. No! It wasn't long after Jacob began working for him that he recognized God's favor was on Jacob. The blessings of the Lord just seemed to pour out of anything Jacob set his hand to. Laban got richer and richer with Jacob working for him. That is why he did everything he could to keep Jacob in his employ.

Unfortunately for Laban, after Jacob married Rachel all he could think about was getting out from under Laban's control. He quickly made the following declaration.

> Give me my wives and my children, for whom I have served thee, and let me go: for thou knowest my service which I have done thee.
>
> And Laban said unto him, I pray thee, if I have found favour in thine eyes, tarry: for I have learned by experience that the Lord hath blessed me for thy sake.
>
> And he said, Appoint me thy wages, and I will give it.
>
> And he said unto him, Thou knowest how I have served thee, and how thy cattle was with me.
>
> For it was little which thou hadst before I came, and it is now increased unto a multitude; and the Lord hath blessed thee since my coming: and now when shall I provide for mine own house also?
>
> Genesis 30:26-30

Jacob said, "Look, I've blessed you and you are very wealthy. Now please allow me to provide for my own family and go." And then Jacob outlined his plan.

> He said, What shall I give thee? And Jacob said, Thou shalt not give me any thing: if thou wilt do this thing for me, I will again feed and keep thy flock:
>
> I will pass through all thy flock to day, removing from thence all the speckled and spotted cattle, and all the brown cattle among the sheep, and the spotted and speckled among the goats: and of such shall be my hire.
>
> Genesis 30:31-32

In other words, Jacob's paycheck was going to be all the spotted and speckled cattle, brown sheep, and spotted and speckled goats. These were rare because cattle and goats normally are born with a solid color, and sheep are normally white. Laban immediately agreed, thinking to himself, *He'll get only a few, and I'll be left with almost everything!* Then he moved away from Jacob and all of his speckled, spotted, and brown livestock.

> Jacob took him rods of green poplar, and of the hazel and chesnut tree; and pilled white strakes in them, and made the white appear which was in the rods.
>
> And he set the rods which he had pilled before the flocks in the gutters in the watering troughs when the flocks came to drink, that they should conceive when they came to drink.
>
> And the flocks conceived before the rods, and brought forth cattle ringstraked, speckled, and spotted.
>
> And Jacob did separate the lambs, and set the faces of the flocks toward the ringstraked, and all the brown in the flock of Laban; and he put his own flocks by themselves, and put them not unto Laban's cattle.
>
> And it came to pass, whensoever the stronger cattle did conceive, that Jacob laid the rods before the eyes of the cattle in the gutters, that they might conceive among the rods.
>
> But when the cattle were feeble, he put them not in: so the feebler were Laban's, and the stronger Jacob's.
>
> And the man increased exceedingly, and had much cattle, and maidservants, and menservants, and camels, and asses.
>
> Genesis 30:37-43

Jacob got richer and richer by placing rods in front of the stronger livestock as they were mating.

> He heard the words of Laban's sons, saying, Jacob hath taken away all that was our father's; and of that which was our father's hath he gotten all this glory.
>
> Genesis 31:1

Here is what I want you to see from this true story. Jacob knew that it wasn't God's will for him to continue to work for Laban. He also knew God loved him and wanted him to go back to his father, Isaac, with his two wives, all his children, and a great fortune. He believed that God would do a miracle to get him away from Laban; he just didn't know how. To expand Jacob's believing and to get Jacob into the impossible, God gave him a dream.

> It came to pass at the time that the cattle conceived, that I lifted up mine eyes, and saw in a dream, and, behold, the rams which leaped upon the cattle were ringstraked, speckled, and grisled.
>
> And the angel of God spake unto me in a dream, saying, Jacob: And I said, Here am I.
>
> And he said, Lift up now thine eyes, and see, all the rams which leap upon the cattle are ringstraked, speckled, and grisled: for I have seen all that Laban doeth unto thee.
>
> Genesis 31:10-12

Jacob woke up and meditated upon the dream. God had told him He would prosper him and deliver him despite Laban's evil schemes. So Jacob pondered it and thought about it day and night. He saw nothing but spotted and speckled calves and goat kids and brown lambs.

When we meditate in God's Word day and night we get His wisdom. Jacob looked around and saw the poplar and chestnut trees, and began to make rods from their branches. Personally, I believe that when he chipped the bark off the branches of those trees and made rods of them, then placed those rods by the water troughs, something in the way those rods looked and smelled caused the livestock to mate. Then Jacob's faith released the Holy Spirit to bring forth spotted, speckled, and brown offspring.

Jacob got into the impossible because he meditated on the Word of God. He was able to control the mating season and override the natural laws of heredity and reproduction. His faith released God to do one miracle after another. This is what God wants for us too!

Sometimes God will give us a spiritual dream or vision like He did Jacob, but in the meantime we can increase our ability to believe by simply meditating in His Word day and night. Keeping our minds renewed is the key to seeing the impossible happen in our lives.

PETER WALKS INTO IMPOSSIBILITY

The boat was already a long distance from the land, battered by the waves; for the wind was contrary.
And in the fourth watch of the night He came to them, walking on the sea.

When the disciples saw Him walking on the sea, they were terrified, and said, "It is a ghost!" And they cried out in fear.

But immediately Jesus spoke to them, saying, "Take courage, it is I; do not be afraid."

Matthew 14:24-27

The disciples were in the boat in the middle of the Sea of Galilee, and a terrible storm rose up to sink them and kill them all. Then they saw Jesus walking on the water toward them, and they really freaked out! They thought He was a ghost, but Jesus said, "Don't be afraid, gentlemen. It's Me."

Peter said to Him, "Lord, if it is You, command me to come to You on the water."

And He said, "Come!" And Peter got out of the boat, and walked on the water and came toward Jesus.

Matthew 14:28-29 NASB

Peter said, "Okay Lord, if it is really You, tell me to come to You out there on the water." I believe that's what God is calling for the church to do right now. He wants us to step out of our comfort zones, crash through those old boundaries and limitations, and walk on the water in *koinonia* with Him! As for me and my house, I'm through rowing! I'm ready to get out of the boat and walk in the reality that nothing is impossible to me if I just believe.

Seeing the wind, he became frightened, and beginning to sink, he cried out, "Lord, save me!"

Immediately Jesus stretched out His hand and took hold of him, and said to him, "You of little faith, why did you doubt?"

Matthew 14:30-31 NASB

Peter walked out on the water, did okay for a while, and then began to sink. Now we have been taught that the reason Peter sank was because he took his eyes off of Jesus, but he sank because his thoughts turned to his physical environment. His mind went to meditating on images of his being engulfed by the waves when he should have maintained the image of him walking on the water with Jesus.

That's what we do. We leave the church full of faith and walking on water with Jesus. We believe we can accomplish all these great things. Then we take a couple steps of faith and our relatives remind us that no one in our family has ever gone to college or started their own business or had a marriage that was happy and lasted a lifetime. We open a magazine or newspaper and there's an article on people like us, and the statistics are not good! That's when we start to sink.

Thank God we have a Lord and Savior who always reaches down to catch us and raise us back up to safety! And we have the Holy Spirit living inside us to remind us to stop thinking those negative, worldly thoughts and get our minds back on God's Word. In a moment's time, we can get back into the impossible by getting our thoughts back on God's powerful, life-transforming Word.

You are made to walk with Jesus—on water! You are made to talk with Him, to think like He thinks, and to act like Him. He's waiting for you to be so filled with His Word and so transformed that you can walk in His supernatural, miracle-working power all day and all night. So get out of that boat and get into the impossible by meditating in His Word!

CHAPTER 12

WOULD YOU BE A KING?

I beseech you therefore, brethren, by the mercies of God, that you present your bodies a living sacrifice, holy, acceptable unto God, which is your reasonable service.

And be not conformed to this world: but be ye transformed by the renewing of your mind, that ye may prove what is that good, and acceptable, and perfect, will of God.

Romans 12:1-2

We have discussed the fact that being conformed means to be squeezed into somebody else's mold, and in verse 2 we are not to be squeezed into the world's mold. We are to be conformed only to the image of Jesus.

For those whom He foreknew, He also predestined to become conformed to the image of His Son, so that He would be the firstborn among many brethren.

Romans 8:29 NASB

The way we are to be conformed to the image of Jesus is to be transformed by the renewing of our minds with the Word of

God. Being transformed is a monumental, radical, and revolutionary change. It is like the transformer toys my son used to play with, and there was recently a movie about them. They would look like cars or trucks or tanks, but when you moved some parts around they turned into supermen or super robots.

We are to replace our old, worldly thinking with God's truth and become supermen and superwomen. As new creatures in Christ Jesus, we are literally a new species of human beings. We walk in the Spirit, not the flesh; we walk in God's wisdom and power. And we have a love for our fellow human beings and particularly for the saints of God that transcends the human, conditional love of the world.

But there's more...

A KING'S MENTALITY

Fight the good fight of faith, lay hold on eternal life, whereunto thou art also called, and hast professed a good profession before many witnesses.

I give thee charge in the sight of God, who quickeneth all things, and before Christ Jesus, who before Pontius Pilate witnessed a good confession;

That thou keep this commandment without spot, unrebukeable, until the appearing of our Lord Jesus Christ:

Which in his times he shall shew, who is the blessed and only Potentate, the King of kings, and Lord of lords;

Who only hath immortality, dwelling in the light which no man can approach unto; whom no man hath seen, nor can see: to whom be honour and power everlasting. Amen.

1 Timothy 6:12-16

If Jesus is the King of kings, who do you think those other kings are? In Chapter 9 we understood from the Word of God that we are the "little gods" under the authority of our big God. Now we read that we are also kings, so our minds must be renewed to the full understanding of our position in God. Only then will we be able to prove in our lives what is "that good and acceptable and perfect will of God."

We were born again out of Egypt (the corrupt, sinful world) where we had a slave mentality. We were locked into a self-image that was limited and bound by how the world had programmed us. We were conformed to the world's system. Now we must throw out that programming and believe what God says about us in His Word. We must live as citizens of Heaven and kings of Earth.

To get us to see who we are and what we are capable of achieving in Him, we have seen how God leads us into the wilderness. There is nothing in the wilderness, and we must live in the supernatural, miracle power of God to survive. We must rely on His grace and love as we choose to believe, confess, and act upon His Word. And we must learn to walk in the Spirit instead of making decisions from our natural reasoning and carnal thinking. In short, our lives become all about Him and His ability instead of us and our ability.

In the wilderness the children of Israel experienced daily miracles just to drink, eat, stay cool during the day and warm during the night. Can you imagine a miracle every day for forty years? This was God's way of saying, "You can trust Me. I'll take good care of you." The ones who came to believe Him were the ones who entered the Promised Land. They didn't see themselves as slaves and grasshoppers. They saw themselves as kings of the land God had given them.

As New Testament believers, God has something greater to say to us in our wilderness. "And by the way, you are supernatural beings with the authority and power of Jesus' name, His blood, and My Word backing you up. You are kings in My Kingdom. You are more than conquerors, and I will always cause you to triumph." (See Romans 8:37 and 2 Corinthians 2:14.)

Whatever God has for us is impossible for us to obtain in our own wisdom and strength. Just as the children of Israel faced the walls of Jericho, we are challenged with insurmountable odds and obstacles as we step out in faith to do what God has called us to do. This might be everything from overcoming an addiction to raising someone from the dead. The only way we are going to succeed is to begin to see ourselves as God sees us.

We must rid ourselves of any part of our previous slave mentality and only receive what His Word says about us. When we have a biblical understanding of who we are in Jesus Christ, we can go into our Promised Land to receive all God has for us. We must be convinced Jericho's walls and all those giants are no match for the wisdom and power of our Father God who loves us.

Kings refuse to allow anyone or anything to label them, put them in a box, or place their values and standards upon them. They believe all things are possible with God, and nothing is too hard for Him.

A king's mentality is triumph in all situations..

LIVING LIKE A KING

After years of reading, studying, and meditating in God's Word, I know who I am. If someone comes up to me and says, "Who are you, Bill Winston?" I will say without hesitation, "I am a king. I am a king because God says I am a king." Years ago I could never have said this. This statement would have been completely out of my comfort zone. But that was before my mind had been renewed with the truth.

As I began to understand what it means to be God's child, that I was a king in His Kingdom, the way I saw myself and the way I conducted my life began to change radically. My outside began to reflect my inside. One day I told my wife, "You know, Sweetheart, I like to drink hot drinks out of a nice china cup."

She looked at me like, *What is this?* That is because it was such a radical change for me. But that radical change was coming from the radical change on the inside of me. There was something in me that knew who I was—a king in God's Kingdom.

A king doesn't get down and dirty if he is God's man. He is kind and sociable, and he conducts himself in a dignified manner. Have you ever seen a good king or queen cursing people out? When we think of kings and queens, the images are majestic and powerful. And have you ever known a king who was poor and barely making it? Furthermore, their children grow up knowing they are royalty. They walk confidently in the power and authority and prosperity of their royal family.

As children of God who are His kings, we come from all walks of life. Some of us are born into the Kingdom of God while we are living in poverty and lack. Some of us come from middle class families that accept the fact that they work hard, sometimes several jobs, and yet never seem to get ahead. Then others come to God having grown up with a silver spoon in their mouths. Yet all of us can enter the Kingdom of God with the idea that money is the root of all evil. But that's not what the Bible says. It is the love of money that is the root of all evil (see 1 Timothy 6:10).

Our natural birth and experiences are not cancelled out at the new birth, and they can keep us from our divine destiny if we let them. We must all get our minds renewed! Romans 8:28 says that God works everything to our good, so He will take our past and our circumstances and use them for His and our benefit. We cannot lose in Jesus Christ! He always causes us to triumph in Him—if our minds are renewed to think like He does.

In order to use our past and our circumstances for our good and His glory, we must stop living like natural human beings and begin living like supernatural human beings, like kings! If we continue living in the natural with God, making decisions based on what our physical senses and the world tell us instead of by the Word and the Spirit, we are not going to do anything for Him.

God is calling every one of us to live the high life, the royal life, the kingly life in Him.

> If because of one man's trespass (lapse, offense) death reigned through that one, much more surely will those who receive [God's] overflowing grace (unmerited favor) and the free gift of righteousness [putting them into right standing with Himself] reign as kings in life through the one Man Jesus Christ (the Messiah, the Anointed One).
>
> Romans 5:17 AMP

The Scripture says that we shall "reign in life as kings." We receive abundance of grace, the free gift of righteousness, and reign as kings from the moment we are born again.

Do you see who you are in Christ Jesus? You are a king!

Stop accepting what other people say about you that is contrary to what God says about you. Believe what the Bible says and be who you were created to be. Then you will be able to do what God called you to do. The world no longer tells you who you are and what your life is and will be. As a king and God's child, you cannot settle for less than what He has for you.

If you are a king under the Most High God, you won't accept certain things like waste, disorder, and confusion—especially when you are the authority over that situation. For example, from time to time I will do spot checks in different areas of the ministry I oversee. I show up when nobody thinks I'm coming. One day I showed up someplace (I won't tell you where!) and what I saw was a mess. As a king, I looked at this mess and said, "How can anybody come in here and stay longer than two seconds?"

God's kings keep their personal kingdoms in order. They are good stewards over all He has given them, and my ministry is part of what He has given me to steward in this Earth. So I supervised some cleanup and reorganization that day. Even if you do not have much materially, you can be neat and clean with what you have. You can show respect and gratitude for what you have been given, and it's easier to believe God for more when you are doing the best you can with what you've got.

When I was a little boy, my mother used to take my brother and sister and me to the country to stay with my grandmother. She lived on a dirt road, in a nice little house, and the yard was dirt, not grass. We would just take a broom and sweep the yard to make it look real neat. Even though she didn't have much, everything was always clean and orderly, and to the day she died she would not let us sit in her living room! She covered that furniture with a sheet, and nobody saw it but really special company. My grandmother was the queen of her home, and when we were in her home we knew it!

THE IMPACT OF GOD'S KINGS

Our church named our business school the Joseph School of Business and Entrepreneurship because Joseph saw himself as a king. He never lost sight of who he was, no matter what his circumstances. God gave him a powerful dream when he was a young man, and that dream determined his destiny. In it God showed him that one day his family and whole nations would bow down to him. From that moment on Joseph saw himself as someone God had called to reign in life.

Joseph believed and trusted God's Word when his brothers ripped his clothes off, threw him in a pit, and sold him into slavery. He continued in faith when Potiphar's wife lied about him and he ended up in prison. Even after years in the dungeon and wondering if people had forgotten him, he knew God had not forgotten him. He persevered in faith and believed God would deliver him—because he knew he was destined to reign.

Finally the day came when Joseph was summoned to Pharaoh. God gave him the wisdom to interpret Pharaoh's dreams, and he was made the prime minister of Egypt. Joseph became the chief financial officer of the greatest nation on the Earth at that time! It wasn't long before his father and his brothers also bowed down to him. The dream God planted in Joseph's heart finally came to pass.

Joseph was bold and confident as God's king, and we should be also.

> Herein is our love made perfect, that we may have boldness in the day of judgment: because as he is, so are we in this world.
>
> 1 John 4:17

This verse is talking about Jesus, the King of kings. We are to be like Him in this world, and He was confident and bold as He walked this Earth.

From Jesus Christ, who is the faithful witness, and the first begotten of the dead, and the prince of the kings of the earth. Unto him that loved us, and washed us from our sins in his own blood,

And hath made us kings and priests unto God and his Father; to him be glory and dominion for ever and ever. Amen.

Revelation 1:5-6

When God taps one of his kings on the shoulder and says, "It's time to take the Promised Land," they don't get this confused, scared look on their face and say, "But I can't afford it! I don't have the education! My mama never married my daddy! I've got too much baggage! I'm not strong enough, good enough, or wise enough to do this!"

Godly kings say, "I trust You, Lord. What's my first step?"

When believers know who they are in Jesus Christ they do not hesitate to follow the leading of the Holy Spirit and trust God's Word in whatever He is calling them to do. Because their minds are being transformed by God's Word, they know to step out in faith and just do it!

Kings are designed by God to defeat the enemy, conquer the land, and rule and reign in His authority, wisdom, and compassion. And when the saints of God wake up to this kingly position He has placed them in and begin to walk in it as the supernatural beings they were created to be, the world is going to be supernaturally impacted with the saving, healing, delivering power of Jesus Christ.

CHAPTER 13

RENEWED MINDS
ARE SOUND MINDS

God hath not given us the spirit of fear; but of power, and
of love, and of a sound mind.

2 Timothy 1:7

Perhaps the greatest benefit of having a mind that is
renewed by the Word of God is that it becomes sound,
which means we are grounded in the truth and free of all
fear. Satan's world system runs on fear, and God's Kingdom
runs on faith, so our transformation is real when we cease
to be afraid of anything the devil can dish out.

God is looking for a people who will not fear, who will
reject all worry, anxiety, and trepidation that comes their
way. Jesus is building a church that will go where the Spirit
says to go and do what the Word says to do knowing their
God is greater than anything or anyone that would oppose
them. The Bride of Christ is a fearless and faithful bride!

Where the devil and his demons are concerned, we need to know exactly where we stand. If we don't stand in the truth that Jesus stripped them of all power and authority over us, they will strip us! Personally, I'm out to strip them of everything they have stolen from me and all who concern me. I won't stop until I see them streaking down the road with nothing on! In the past we have let them rob us of our marriages, our children, our friends, our jobs, our gifts and callings, our health, and our joy and peace. No more! I am determined that they will return seven-fold what they have stolen from us and never steal from us again.

You cannot have this kind of aggressive attitude toward the enemy without having a renewed mind. You must be rooted and grounded in God's love and truth to be a light in this world, to do your part in the body of Christ, to reach out to the lost and disciple the nations.

OUR ROLE AS FEARLESS PRIESTS

From Jesus Christ, who is the faithful witness, and the first begotten of the dead, and the prince of the kings of the earth. Unto him that loved us, and washed us from our sins in his own blood,

And hath made us kings and priests unto God and his Father; to him be glory and dominion for ever and ever. Amen.

Revelation 1:5-6

We are not only kings but also priests to our God. Jesus Christ is our High Priest (Hebrews 2:17), and we are His priestly representatives on Earth.

What do priests do? Priests worship the Lord with all their hearts and lives, and they are mediators between the Lord and people who don't know Him. A king stands before the people for God, but a priest stands before God for the people and leads the people into His presence. These roles speak of our purpose: to have dominion and to make disciples of all nations.

People around the world are living in the shadow of terrorism, and we know that Jesus is their only hope to overcome all fear and defeat the enemy. Ever since 9-11 the United States has been consumed with security and safety issues, and the church should be the beacon of light in this frightening darkness. People need our faith and our confidence in the Lord to protect them. And they need to hear the Good News! There is nothing but bad news on television and radio, except for the preachers and teachers of the Gospel who are saying, "Hey, we serve a loving and all-powerful Heavenly Father who is greater than any terrorist out there. He knows where every one of those guys is and what they are planning, so we just need to stick with Him."

Now is the time to say, "Come on over to my house and hear about Jesus. You can have His peace and know He is protecting you. I know things are frightening out there, but in your heart you can have joy. You can have a sound mind that knows the truth."

If you can't say that and believe it, you need to get your mind renewed fast!

Today is harvest time. We have tremendous opportunities to lead people to the Lord and show them the great truths from the Bible that will change them and transform them into the people they were created to be. Then they can go out and do the same thing with others who need Jesus. This is what God wants us to do as His priests. But our minds must be renewed and our lives transformed in order to walk in and be the light in this dark and terrifying world.

WHEN FEAR ATTACKS

All the congregation lifted up their voice, and cried; and the people wept that night.

And all the children of Israel murmured against Moses and against Aaron: and the whole congregation said unto them, Would God that we had died in the land of Egypt! or would God we had died in this wilderness!

And wherefore hath the Lord brought us unto this land, to fall by the sword, that our wives and our children should be a prey? were it not better for us to return into Egypt?

And they said one to another, Let us make a captain, and let us return into Egypt.

Numbers 14:1-4

What's happening to the children of Israel in these verses? Fear! Fear's coming in to stop them, and fear did stop them from entering the Promised Land. They had left the ghetto and God was getting ready to move them into the mansions those giants had built for them when they allowed fear to grab them by their throats. They were so afraid that they wanted to go back to the ghetto!

When you believe the evil report, the report that opposes what God's Word has said and what the Holy Spirit has told you, then you will do the craziest things. Why? Because you do not have a sound mind. Your mind is not renewed by God's Word, and so you become vulnerable to fear and every deception of the enemy. Always remember, the enemy is out to destroy you. If he can't destroy you, then he will attempt to deceive you and keep you from everything God has for you in Jesus Christ.

Sound minds believe only God's Word. They follow only the Holy Spirit. And they are fearless and aggressive when it comes to the enemy. They don't wait around for him to show up and attack. They move forward in the power and authority of God's Word as though he didn't even exist. When he does show up, they just get rid of him!

THE FIRST RULE OF WARFARE: NO FEAR

When thou goest out to battle against thine enemies, and seest horses, and chariots, and a people more than thou, be not afraid of them: for the Lord thy God is with thee, which brought thee up out of the land of Egypt.

Deuteronomy 20:1

The first rule of warfare, spiritual or physical, is to "be not afraid." Remember, the devil needs fear to control people like God needs faith to move in and through His people. Hebrews 11:1 tells us that "faith is the substance of things hoped for, the evidence of things not seen." If faith is the substance of things hoped for, then fear is the substance of things you don't want!

Job said, "The thing which I greatly feared is come upon me, and that which I was afraid of is come unto me" (Job 3:25). Because Job allowed fear to dominate him instead of having faith in God, the devil robbed him of his children, his livestock, his servants, and his friends. The moment he gave in to fear, the enemy came in to steal everything he could steal.

When the enemy shows up it is not time to fear; it is time to fight the good fight of faith! When your mind is renewed to what God has promised and what He has given you, you can fight and win over any strategy and plan of the devil. Your renewed, sound mind will think like Jesus, your Commander-in-Chief, and the Holy Spirit will tell you exactly what to do to get the victory.

If your mind has not been renewed to what God's Word says, then you will follow right along with the all the others who are scared out of their minds—literally! You can be born again, but if your mind is not renewed you can be afraid to fly on an airplane, afraid to send your kids to school, and even afraid to go out of your house.

The Bible is very clear that fear is not an option in war.

It shall be, when ye are come nigh unto the battle, that the priest shall approach and speak unto the people,

And shall say unto them, Hear, O Israel, ye approach this day unto battle against your enemies: let not your hearts faint, fear not, and do not tremble, neither be ye terrified because of them;

For the Lord your God is he that goeth with you, to fight for you against your enemies, to save you.

Deuteronomy 20:2-3

The priest got in everybody's face and commanded them not to be afraid of the enemy. As priests of God, we are to encourage one another in the faith and help each other defeat fear in our lives. There is no room for fear in the body of Christ! Our knees may start shaking, but that's the same as a headache coming on us. What do we do with a headache? We rebuke it! We war against it in the name of Jesus, and we do the same with fear.

As priests we are also to tell the unbelievers in our lives about the saving, delivering grace of Jesus Christ. We are to boldly proclaim that if they trust in Him and are born again, they will never have to live in fear again. This passage of Scripture in Deuteronomy says that the Lord will go with all of us and fight for us. He will save us from our enemies. That means He will give us victory, deliver us fully, and rescue us from anything and anyone the devil sends against us. That's the Good News the world is desperate to hear!

FAITH AND FEAR ARE CONTAGIOUS

The officers shall speak further unto the people, and they shall say, What man is there that is fearful and faint-hearted? let him go and return unto his house, lest his brethren's heart faint as well as his heart.

Deuteronomy 20:8

God commanded the officers to find out who was afraid and send them home! That would be like a platoon sergeant standing before his outfit, demanding, "Who's chicken?" If you were afraid, you would have to go home because the military would not be successful with fearful soldiers on the front lines. They need men and women who are "strong and of a good courage" (Joshua 1:6-9), those who will be full of faith that God is true to His Word.

Another reason those who are afraid must go home is because fear is contagious. That's why the enemy loves to broadcast evil reports on television and radio and the Internet. He loves to get the rumors flying and bind us up with so much fear that we can't do anything for God. And when a battle arises, if we look at the brothers and sisters and see nothing but terror on their faces, chances are we are going to make a run for it!

Do you know it is possible to have thousands of saints together, all praying the Word, and nothing happens because they are all in fear? There is no faith for God to move in. Zero faith brings zero results. And I've seen believers lose faith for the dumbest reasons. One man came into a church for prayer and insisted that only Deacon Jones could pray for him. When he was asked why, he said, "Because Deacon Jones got some strong prayer."

The truth was, Deacon Jones was a strong prayer warrior all right, but so were all the other deacons. The only difference was that Deacon Jones prayed louder than any of the other deacons! So this man's faith really rested not in the Word and the Spirit of God but in the volume of someone's prayers.

Volume does not signify faith. I've watched some believers whisper God's Word and the devil left the premises. All God needs is our faith to do what He's got to do. And the more saints who agree and pray in faith, the more He can accomplish. You see, fear is not the only thing that is contagious. Faith is also contagious. That's why the Bible tells us to fellowship with each other. Spending time with folks who are full of faith will get us full of faith and keep us full of faith. Our minds will become more and more sound and stable.

On the other hand, if we hang around unbelievers or believers who are not renewing their minds with God's Word, we risk polluting our minds and opening ourselves up to fear and unbelief because their fear and anxiety are contagious. We can witness to unbelievers and try to encourage backsliders to get into God's Word and renew their minds, but the minute we feel our sound mind beginning to slip into fear and doubt, we need to flee that place and get back into fellowship with faith-filled saints.

FEAR DISTORTS THE TRUTH

When you become afraid, the truth about everything in your life is distorted. First of all, you have a distorted image of God. You see Him as a judge who is waiting for you to mess up and is always mad at you. You see Him as a hard taskmaster who wants to teach you through severe suffering. He wants to punish you for sinning and make you sick to chastise you.

This deceptive view of God and His character leads you right into a distortion of how you see yourself. You no longer see yourself as the precious child God loves or believe you are righteous and holy in His eyes. Instead, you are never good enough for Him, and failure is your middle name. Whenever you do sin or make a mistake, like Adam and Eve after the Fall, you hide from God and try to cover your nakedness. You are thinking like a fallen human being because your mind is not renewed with God's Word. You are looking to your own actions instead of Jesus to save you.

Fear has completely perverted your judgment, and it also destroys your relationships. Because you have a distorted view of God and yourself, you have a distorted view of others around you. You will go from church to church trying to find acceptance from people you don't love or trust, because if you don't love and trust God or yourself, how are you going to love or trust anyone else?

Fear also severely impairs your decision-making ability. When you are too scared even to make a decision, you will procrastinate. "Oh well, I'll wait until next time," and then next time never comes. You are paralyzed and unable to move forward in anything God is calling you to do.

Being bit by fear is like being bit by a snake. The venom of fear flows through your body and your mind sees everything out of proportion. Eventually you can't move at all. Fear can also squeeze the life out of you, like a boa constrictor. It wraps itself around you until you cannot move, and then it devours you. The Bible says that the devil is always seeking someone to devour.

> Be sober, be vigilant; because your adversary the devil, as a roaring lion, walketh about, seeking whom he may devour.
>
> 1 Peter 5:8

Fear hinders all the creative gifts and talents God has given you. You're afraid people will think you aren't good enough or that you will be publicly humiliated and make a fool of yourself. Because you are locked into fear instead of faith, the supernatural power of God is cut off in your life and you have a hard time hearing from Him. Your mind is so filled with anxious images and thoughts that you cannot hear the gentle voice and receive the awesome comfort of the Holy Spirit inside your spirit.

It is very hard to hear from God when fear grips your soul because your mind was created to be in a condition of faith, not fear. At the new birth you were given a spirit of faith (2 Corinthians 4:13). Your entire being is designed to operate by faith, walking in the supernatural power of God and doing mighty exploits. In short, you are to do the very works that Jesus did—miracles, signs, and wonders.

In 1 Peter 5:8 it says we are to be sober and vigilant. What are we to be sober and vigilant about? Renewing our minds with God's Word! Only by keeping our minds renewed with God's Word will we have a sound mind that will defeat fear at every turn of our lives, enable us to hear the Holy Spirit, and walk in the miracle-working power of God.

A Prayer to Keep a Sound Mind

If you have struggled with fear, and I believe all of us at one time or another have to contend with fear, then I encourage you to pray this prayer out loud every day until you get the victory over it.

"Father, from this day forward I fear no evil, no enemy, no terrorist, and no attacks of the devil. Fear, in the name of Jesus I command you to leave my mind, my emotions, and my body. I am off limits to all fear because I am the right-eousness of God in Christ Jesus. His blood has washed me clean, I am a king and priest unto God, and as His beloved I am as bold as a lion. I fear nothing—no person, no religion, no witchcraft, no sickness, and no poverty! This day is a new day in which I walk in complete faith and trust in God and His Word. In Jesus' mighty name I pray, amen."

When fear attacks you, treat it like profanity or lying or stealing or any other sin. I also suggest you memorize Psalm 91 and say it out loud often, but especially during times of great stress. This Psalm has kept many saints of God safe in situations where they should have perished.

Always remember, God has not given you a spirit of fear. He has given you an eternal spirit filled with His Spirit, and along with that comes a sound mind—a mind that is being redesigned by His Holy Word to know absolutely and unequivocally that nothing is too great for God.

CHAPTER 14

GOING THROUGH THE FIRE

I beseech you therefore, brethren, by the mercies of God, that ye present your bodies a living sacrifice, holy, acceptable unto God, which is your reasonable service.

And be not conformed to this world: but be ye transformed by the renewing of your mind, that you may prove what is that good, and acceptable, and perfect, will of God.

Romans 12:1-2

What is the purpose of having a renewed mind? Why does God command us to be transformed by His Word? It is because He wants us to prove His good, acceptable, and perfect will. Our God is a big God and He wants to do big things in us, for us, and through us. But He cannot lead us where we cannot see. He cannot move past the strength of our faith. Therefore, He has to expand our capacity to see and believe so that we will walk into the impossible and He can perform miracles, signs, and wonders in and through our lives.

Doesn't this sound fantastic? Don't you want to renew your mind day and night, just like God instructed Joshua in Joshua 1:8, so that you will have great success in all you do? But think again. What happens to people who have great faith and believe that all things are possible with God? They find themselves standing in front of a heavily armed giant with only a slingshot in their hands! They are caught face-to-face with a bunch of hungry lions in their den. And they are thrown into a furnace that is so hot, the guys who throw them in are vaporized.

Do you still want miracles, signs, and wonders in your life? God created you to say yes!

BE OF A GOOD COURAGE!

God wants to bring a radical transformation in your mind and heart so that you can have supernatural courage in the face of insurmountable odds. The world will say,

"It can't be done."

"It is not humanly possible."

"You're too young."

"You're too old."

"There is no science to support this."

"You are crazy, and everyone around you thinks you're crazy."

"No one will help you. No one will believe you."

"You must accept the facts."

"It is medically proven that this is what will happen."

"If you do this you will put yourself and everyone you know in jeopardy."

"Statistically, you will never get more than a high school education."

"What you want is just not in your gene pool."

"Nobody from your neighborhood has ever done what you want to do."

"You're the wrong color, wrong gender, and from the wrong side of the tracks."

What you need to come to grips with is that miracles, signs, and wonders do not occur unless there is a problem, an obstacle, a crisis, a tragedy, or a catastrophe to deal with. Sometimes God will warn you of impending danger and you will be able to pray it away or avoid it in the natural as a result of His warning. But when He wants to really show up and reveal His power and glory, He usually leads His people into dangerous and terrible situations.

FAITH UNDER FIRE

When we are under pressure, we find out what we really believe. There is the old example of putting a tea bag in hot water. Only in hot water can the tea bag release the flavor and aroma that it contains. We are the same way. Until the Holy Spirit leads us into a tight situation, we cannot release the faith and goodness of God inside us.

Now I know you might be thinking, *But I thought God was a good God who would never put His children in harm's way or set them in the middle of a disaster.* Our God is a good God who promises no harm will come to us *even when we go through fire and flood.* He did not promise we would never face adversity or go through hard times.

Many are the afflictions of the righteous: but the Lord delivereth him out of them all.

Psalm 34:19

No one knew better than David that serving the Lord meant a life of fighting battles of faith. Again and again he fought—and again and again he saw the delivering hand of God bring him and his people through to victory. David understood that faith was true faith when he was under fire. He knew that every time he stood before a giant or an army that outnumbered his army, God was there to show Himself strong.

The three Hebrew boys, Shadrach, Meschach, and Abednego, faced a literal fire when they stood for the

Lord. King Nebuchadnezzar threatened to kill them just because they refused to bow to the statue he had built of himself. In the end the Lord delivered them—but not from the fiery furnace!

> These three men, Shadrach, Meshach, and Abednego, fell down bound into the midst of the burning fiery furnace.
>
> Then Nebuchadnezzar the king was astonied, and rose up in haste, and spake, and said unto his counsellors, Did not we cast three men bound into the midst of the fire? They answered and said unto the king, True, O king.
>
> He answered and said, Lo, I see four men loose, walking in the midst of the fire, and they have no hurt; and the form of the fourth is like the Son of God.
>
> Daniel 3:23-25

Jesus stood there and allowed those boys to be bound up and thrown into that fire, and He was so excited about their faith that He jumped in there with them! Everyone stood and watched in astonishment as Shadrach, Meschach, and Abednego danced with the King of kings and Lord of lords in the midst of that fire. No natural bonds could hold them when they stepped into the fire in faith!

> Then Nebuchadnezzar came near to the mouth of the burning fiery furnace, and spake, and said, Shadrach, Meshach, and Abednego, ye servants of the most high God, come forth, and come hither. Then Shadrach, Meshach, and Abednego, came forth of the midst of the fire.
>
> And the princes, governors, and captains, and the king's counsellors, being gathered together, saw these men, upon whose bodies the fire had no power, nor was an hair

of their head singed, neither were their coats changed, nor the smell of fire had passed on them.

Daniel 3:26-27

This miracle had an incredible impact upon the king and his entire kingdom. Those three boys came out of the fire, and not a hair on their head was singed! They didn't even smell like smoke. A nation was changed because of the faith of these three young men in their God.

> Then Nebuchadnezzar spake, and said, Blessed be the God of Shadrach, Meshach, and Abednego, who hath sent his angel, and delivered his servants that trusted in him, and have changed the king's word, and yielded their bodies, that they might not serve nor worship any god, except their own God.
>
> Therefore I make a decree, That every people, nation, and language, which speak any thing amiss against the God of Shadrach, Meshach, and Abednego, shall be cut in pieces, and their houses shall be made a dunghill: because there is no other God that can deliver after this sort.

Daniel 3:28-29

A king and his entire empire turned to the God of Shadrach, Meschach, and Abednego because they kept the faith in the midst of adversity. So the next time you find yourself in a really tough situation, turn to Jesus and ask Him if it's time to do that victory dance in the fire! You will be a powerful witness of God's love and power to everyone who sees you face your adversity in faith.

INTIMIDATION

How did Shadrach, Meschach, and Abednego do what they did? Remember, these boys weren't born again. They didn't have the Holy Spirit living inside them. And they didn't have the New Testament to study and meditate upon. They just had some of the Old Testament, but they renewed their minds with that, and something amazing happened. Because they honored God's Word, He sent the Living Word to dance in the fire with them. Those boys got a revelation of Jesus Christ as their deliverer that not many New Covenant believers have had!

If Old Testament believers like Moses, David, Daniel, and Shadrach, Meschach, and Abednego could do great exploits like this, why can't we? After all, we have more Word and the Holy Spirit living inside us. We should be running rings around what the Old Testament saints did. What is our problem?

Mostly, I believe we are intimidated by the enemy. You are probably thinking, *I'm not afraid of the devil. I have authority over him in Jesus' name.* But do you recognize the devil in the systems of this world? Do you see his evil handiwork in the political system, the economic system, the educational system, or the entertainment system? When you talk politics with your unsaved neighbor, do you hesitate to state your beliefs? Or maybe you just stopped voting altogether because you are so fed up with the system.

What about economics? There are all kinds of news programs and articles about how difficult it is to get ahead and realize the American Dream today. The value of the American dollar has fallen drastically in recent years. We are importing more and exporting less. Does that make you anxious for yourself or your children?

We don't have to say much about the entertainment system because their agenda is so obvious. We encounter everything from perversion to witchcraft in movies, television, books, magazines, and all over the Internet. Does that overwhelm you and make you want to just hide in your home until Jesus comes back?

Then there is the educational system, which has been working for decades in this country to systematically turn students of all ages away from God and the Bible to secular thought and belief. More and more children and young adults are emerging from our educational institutions, especially the public ones, with no biblical view whatsoever. Many have never even heard the name Jesus except as a cuss word.

Do you look at all these "giants" and wail like the children of Israel, "We are grasshoppers in their sight?" Or maybe when you come up against them and they command you to bow to their images, you decide to bow rather than to burn. If you are overwhelmed, defeated, and depressed by all these things, then you are allowing the enemy to intimidate you. You have forgotten who you are in Christ Jesus! You are a king, a priest, and a god who represents the Most

High God. You walk in His infallible Word and the power of His Holy Spirit.

You need to learn the joy of your salvation by the renewing of your mind.

COUNT IT ALL JOY!

My brethren, count it all joy when ye fall into divers temptations;

Knowing this, that the trying of your faith worketh patience.

But let patience have her perfect work, that ye may be perfect and entire, wanting nothing.

James 1:2-4

All of us want to get to the place in God where we are "perfect and entire, wanting nothing." We want to have sound minds that are not intimidated or deceived by the enemy. We want to be productive and effective, to have a mighty impact for Jesus Christ in our world. But we have to come to grips with the fact that there's no better witness for the grace, love, and final authority of God than a saint who refuses to bow, gets thrown into the fire, dances the victory dance with Jesus in the flames, and then comes out not even smelling of smoke. Now that is something that is going to get the world's attention!

People sit up and take notice when a believer walks in the power and authority of God, especially when they are under severe pressure. They want what that believer has when they see them shatter the boundaries and limitations the world has placed on them, become successful, and still have peace and joy. They covet their faith and their relationship with God when they see them get healed of a terminal disease or pray their children out of drugs and sexual promiscuity into godly purity and purpose.

From this moment on, before the devil shows up at your door and presents you with a problem as big as the walls of Jericho, as perverse and cunning as the Canaanites, or as strong and arrogant as the sons of Anak, make the decision that you will believe and act only upon God's Word and the leading of His Spirit. Refuse to bow to the evil systems of this world through intimidation or fear. This is what God calls us to do, and He tells us how to do it again and again in the Old and the New Testaments:

> This book of the law shall not depart out of thy mouth; but thou shalt meditate therein day and night, that thou mayest observe to do according to all that is written therein: for then thou shalt make thy way prosperous, and then thou shalt have good success.
>
> Joshua 1:8

> I beseech you therefore, brethren, by the mercies of God, that ye present your bodies a living sacrifice, holy, acceptable unto God, which is your reasonable service.
> And be not conformed to this world: but be ye transformed by the renewing of your mind, that ye may prove what is that good, and acceptable, and perfect, will of God.
>
> Romans 12:1-2

Meditation of God's Word is designed to expand your capacity to receive God's wisdom and power, to make decisions from a level that's consistent with the thinking and ability of God. Meditation is designed to enable you to see that every promise of God is yours, that He withholds no good thing from you. The degree to which you think and see as God thinks and sees is the degree to which you will succeed and prove His will.

Meditation in God's Word turns every trial and tribulation into a mission of joy!

CHAPTER 15

THE LESSONS
OF JERICHO

We have talked about how God will change and transform our thinking through several ways. Sometimes He will bring us through an experience that inspires and motivates us to change the way we think, speak, and act. Sometimes He will give us a dream or a vision that will set our hearts for life, like he did with Joseph. But most of the time He is continuously conforming us to the image of His Son as we allow the Holy Spirit to renew our minds with His Word. In most cases and situations, it is in God's Word that we find the answer, the way of escape, the faith, the confidence, and the courage to overcome, to succeed, and to fight through to the victory.

This is the process God took Joshua through. Joshua was a type of the New Testament believer. He had the example of Moses, the deliverer, who was a type of Jesus. He had the anointing of the Holy Spirit on him. And He had the Word of God, the five books Moses had written—Genesis through Deuteronomy—to meditate in. He had everything he needed to succeed. All he had to do was meditate in God's Word day and night. (See Joshua 1:8.)

MEETING THE CHALLENGE

We have seen how God always calls us to do something we are incapable of doing in our own strength and ability. He presents us with a challenge, and we immediately have a choice to make. We can either lie down and die or get in God's Word, get our thinking transformed, and allow the Holy Spirit to move in us and through us in a supernatural way.

Joshua's first big challenge was the city of Jericho, which was an impregnable fortress surrounded by great walls.

> Now Jericho was straitly shut up because of the children of Israel: none went out, and none came in.
>
> And the Lord said unto Joshua, See, I have given into thine hand Jericho, and the king thereof, and the mighty men of valour.
>
> Joshua 6:1-2

I want you to notice that the Lord said, "I have given...." In the natural Joshua did not possess Jericho, but in the spirit realm the city was already in the possession of the children of Israel. God had given His Word on it. Instead of meditating on the walls and the giants, Joshua meditated on the Word of the Lord.

Meditation brought Joshua's mind and heart into the reality of what God had spoken. He saw that the city was already theirs in the spirit. Therefore, he could act according to what he saw, which was what God had spoken. Meditation in God's Word is the way to meet any challenge.

Meditation in God's Word enables us to visualize and receive in the natural realm what God has already given us in the spiritual realm.

RECEIVING THE PLAN

Something wonderful happens when you get in a tight spot and begin meditating in God's Word. Your Commander-in-Chief begins to give you the battle plan to achieve victory. This is what happened to Joshua when he was facing the formidable walls of Jericho, and this is what will happen to you when you are facing a family crisis, a health issue, a financial burden, or any other challenge in life. As soon as you grab your Bible and begin to read, study, and meditate, the Holy Ghost will speak to you. He will show you the way to go.

> Ye shall compass the city, all ye men of war, and go round about the city once. Thus shalt thou do six days.
>
> And seven priests shall bear before the ark seven trumpets of rams' horns: and the seventh day ye shall compass the city seven times, and the priests shall blow with the trumpets.
>
> And it shall come to pass, that when they make a long blast with the ram's horn, and when ye hear the sound of the

trumpet, all the people shall shout with a great shout; and the wall of the city shall fall down flat, and the people shall ascend up every man straight before him.

Joshua 6:3-5

God didn't ask Joshua to go to the nearest ATM and pull out a couple thousand dollars to pay for Jericho. He gave him wisdom. He didn't give him the wisdom that comes from the fallen human mind; He gave him godly wisdom to receive what was already his. So often we think all we need is money, but what we need is wisdom. Other times we think we have to bargain to get what we need from God when He's already given it to us! All we need is His wisdom, His plan, to receive what He's already given.

If we walk in God's supernatural wisdom, all of our needs will be supernaturally met.

Take another look at what God told Joshua to do. It wasn't a lot. All they had to do was walk around the city and blow the trumpets. That doesn't sound like conventional warfare to me! What was God trying to do here? The only way Joshua could find out was by meditating on God's instructions. As Joshua pondered and muttered all that God said, he began to see the children of Israel marching around those walls once every day for six days. He saw them march around the walls seven times on the seventh day, and he saw the priests blow the trumpets. And then he saw those huge, monumental walls fall flat!

LEADING THE PEOPLE IN MEDITATION

Joshua had commanded the people, saying, Ye shall not shout, nor make any noise with your voice, neither shall any word proceed out of your mouth, until the day I bid you shout; then shall ye shout.

Joshua 6:10

As Joshua meditated on the word of the Lord, he was transformed on the inside to meet the challenge and execute the plan on the outside. And when he imparted God's wisdom and plan to the children of Israel, what do you think they were thinking about and meditating on as they walked silently around Jericho for seven days? With every step their minds were being renewed to the reality that God had given them the city, and nothing could prevent them from taking it.

It is important for us to remember that meditation is not a one-time deal. Meditation is only effective by repetition. Like a cow chewing its cud, we must chew on the Word and chew on the Word, giving the Holy Spirit all the time and opportunity He needs to break it down for us. We must allow Him to bring out all the revelation and wisdom we need to meet the challenges of our lives.

Joshua understood this. He knew the reason God wanted the children of Israel to walk around those walls all those days. The people needed time to meditate and get their minds renewed and their thinking transformed.

> It came to pass on the seventh day, that they rose early about the dawning of the day, and compassed the city after the same manner seven times: only on that day they compassed the city seven times.
>
> And it came to pass at the seventh time, when the priests blew with the trumpets, Joshua said unto the people, Shout; for the Lord hath given you the city.
>
> Joshua 6:15-16

By the seventh day, after walking seven times around Jericho, after meditating God's Word for seven days and nights, how do you think the children of Israel reacted when they heard Joshua cry, "Shout; for the Lord hath given you the city"? By that time they were so filled with faith, they exploded in a supernatural shout that caused those walls to fall down flat!

Great leaders will always give you the word of the Lord and exhort you to meditate in it day and night. They will get the revelation and impart the revelation so that you can run with it and succeed in life.

> The Lord answered me, and said, Write the vision, and make it plain upon tables, that he may run that readeth it.
>
> Habakkuk 2:2

God calls and gives a vision to a leader in the body of Christ, but that leader then has the responsibility to impart that vision and make it plain to those who are called to run with that vision. When we bought the mall, God had a plan and a purpose for it that I imparted to those in my congregation and those who were called to partner with me in this ministry. I gave them the word of the Lord and exhorted them to meditate in it day and night, to water that word with the Word of God, and to pray in the Spirit so that their faith would remain strong.

Joshua wasn't going to take the Promised Land alone, and every leader in the church knows that their success rests in both the power of God and the faithfulness of those who partner with them. I thank God every day for those who labor with us in our ministry, and I do my utmost to impart revelation and feed the sheep so that they can meet every challenge life gives them.

Whatever your vision, God has a plan. You receive that plan by meditating in His Word. And when you follow His plan, His supernatural wisdom and ability are going to see you through to the victory. You cannot fail and you will receive all Jesus died to give you when you are transformed by the renewing of your mind!

FROM WILDERNESS TO PROMISED LAND

When you are born again and begin to meditate in God's Word day and night, you are going from the wilderness into the Promised Land. In the wilderness, God does everything for you. He drew you to Himself. His Holy Spirit convicted you of your sin. You repented of your sin, and He stepped in and brought you out of the kingdom of darkness into His Kingdom of Light. For a while there, He treated you like the baby you were, meeting every need and helping you through every situation.

Then something happens. A challenge presents itself and what worked in the past is not working. You know God's Word has not changed. You know God has not changed. So what is different?

God is calling you to be different!

He is saying, "It's time for you to work *with* Me. I have already given Jericho to you, but I'm not just going to hand it to you. We are going to take it together. You have been restored to relationship with Me, the same relationship Adam and Eve had with Me in the Garden. So we will walk and talk together, and you will learn to walk in My authority and My ways. As you learn to think like Me, you will take dominion over that which I have given you. You will guard it and keep it. And you will be fruitful and multiply in all you do."

Instead of working for *you, God is now working* through *you.*

The children of Israel took every piece of the Promised Land by meditating in God's Word, receiving His wisdom, and following His instructions—and they grew up and were transformed. They became a picture of Jesus Christ in the Earth. Their hearts and minds were filled with who He was and who they were in Him. Therefore, they revealed the God of Abraham, Isaac, and Jacob to the world around them.

Spiritual maturity is moving from the wilderness into the Promised Land.

MY JERICHO

The time came when God brought me to Chicago, and we started the ministry there. Then He told me to go on radio. I went down to the radio station, talked with the station manager, and worked out a deal with him. I came home rejoicing, saying, "Thank You, Jesus, I'm going on radio every Saturday."

At that moment in my spirit I heard Him say as plain as day, "Every Saturday? I don't want you to go on every Saturday. I want you to go on every day."

In the natural there was no way I could afford to be on radio every day. I was suddenly faced with huge walls that I knew I could not conquer in my own strength. What God was asking was impossible.

When God asks the impossible, it's time to renew your mind!

He wants to work with you and through you, but He can work only in the level of your faith, and your faith comes by hearing the Word of God. (See Romans 10:17.) I was tempted to say, "No way! I don't have the money to go on every day. You know I can't afford that."

Thank God I didn't open my mouth and speak this! If I had, I would not have received what God had for me. Instead I went to His Word and began muttering and pondering and chewing on who I was in Christ until I got His mind and His plan. I was transformed and conformed to the image of Jesus more and more. And I went on radio every day! I took my Jericho by meditating in the Word day and night.

WE ARE TO BE LIKE HIM

God said, Let us make man in our image, after our likeness: and let them have dominion over the fish of the sea, and over the fowl of the air, and over the cattle, and over all the earth, and over every creeping thing that creepeth upon the earth.

Genesis 1:26

God always takes you to a land you cannot afford or conquer when He wants to reveal something to you, and that something usually has to do with who you are in Him. You are made in His likeness and image, which means you should think like Him and act like Him. The Hebrew words for "image" and "likeness" are interesting words. In simple terms, if we are made in His image we should look like Him,[1] and if we are in His likeness we should function like He functions.[2]

You have been born again of His Spirit. The same stuff in Him is now in you. You can walk confidently and boldly in His authority and power. He functions by speaking words of faith, so that is how you function in this world. He is a spirit and the Father of spirits (John 4:24 and Hebrews 12:9), so we should function as spiritual beings. We no longer walk according to the flesh, the world, or the enemies of God. We walk by faith according to the Spirit and the Word.

This is the mentality God wants us to get deep down into our subconscious so that when we face another Jericho, who we are and what we have in Him will just rise up and reject any unbelief or doubt or fear that would keep us from receiving all He has for us. He wants us to live in a place we cannot afford, be in health, and be blessed in all our relationships. He wants us to succeed in all we do so that we can prove His will to the people around us.

As the pastor of our church, I've had plenty of opportunities to prove His will! I remember every wall of Jericho I have faced, from buying our first copier to buying a mall. In every situation, only by renewing my mind with God's Word and seeking the wisdom and guidance of the Holy Spirit was I able to do what God called me to do. In order to fulfill my divine destiny, I had to look divine and function in a divine manner! I had to walk in His image and likeness, and the only way to do that was to be transformed by renewing my mind with His Word.

In every situation, at every challenge, I turned to God's Word to meet it and conquer it. When we bought our first church van, which would be used primarily to pick up people in the neighborhoods and bring them to church, I looked at every van on the lot and determined we should buy the least expensive one. Then the Holy Spirit said to me,

"Would you like to ride from here to Ohio in that?" Why He picked Ohio, I have no idea! But that's what He asked me.

I said, "Well, it would be a little hard."

He said, "Go down there and pick out something that is worthy of My people."

In this transaction I got some revelation on how God loves and honors His people, no matter what neighborhood they come from or how much money they have. He showed me a little more about how I am to look and function in His Kingdom, and that is a whole lot different than the world!

I had come from Egypt, where everyone had very little and very few were healthy and happy. But I was finding out that God had a different idea about living life. His Word told me He wanted me to be healthy and happy and blessed. My perception of reality had to change.

There is no end to what God will do for us when we meditate in His Word day and night. We will have success, but more than that, we will come to know who He is and who we are in Him. As our intimacy and knowledge of Him increases, so will our ability to prosper. The following passage of Scripture says it all.

> Grace and peace be multiplied unto you through the knowledge of God, and of Jesus our Lord,
>
> According as his divine power hath given unto us all things that pertain unto life and godliness, through the knowledge of him that hath called us to glory and virtue:

Whereby are given unto us exceeding great and precious promises: that by these ye might be partakers of the divine nature, having escaped the corruption that is in the world through lust.

And beside this, giving all diligence, add to your faith virtue; and to virtue knowledge;

And to knowledge temperance; and to temperance patience; and to patience godliness;

And to godliness brotherly kindness; and to brotherly kindness charity.

For if these things be in you, and abound, they make you that ye shall neither be barren nor unfruitful in the knowledge of our Lord Jesus Christ.

2 Peter 1:2-8

Never barren or unfruitful in Jesus Christ! You will always be blessed and succeed in the knowledge of the Lord. As you meditate in that knowledge, you will receive the grace and peace you need to meet every challenge and conquer every Jericho you face. His divine power has already given you everything you need and desire, and as you stand on His promise the greatest miracle occurs. You partake of His divine nature and become more and more like Him!

CHAPTER 16

PERCEPTION BECOMES REALITY

As he thinketh in his heart, so is he.

Proverbs 23:7

What are you thinking?

Are you thinking about something that's true? That's real?

Are you thinking about something that is pure fantasy?

Are you thinking about something that's sinful? Evil?

Are you thinking about something that's lovely, a good report, of virtue?

You are what you think. You become what you think. And that is why the apostle Paul begs you to learn to think like God. If you think like God, you will be like God, and you will do what God would do in any given situation.

You decide what is going to be real to you. You make choices, every moment of every day, that either bring your thinking into line with God's Word and therefore God's thinking or bring your thinking into conformity with the devil, the world, and your flesh. You determine whether or not you will be like Jesus by what you choose to think about.

EXAMINE YOUR BELIEF SYSTEM

We've talked about the fact that we don't see *with* our eyes; we see *through* our eyes. Our minds, what we believe, determine what we actually see. It is what we perceive to be true that becomes the reality of our lives. It is what you believe you see that you see.

Your belief system has been shaped and molded by all the significant people in your life: your parents, your teachers, your coaches, your music and art instructors, your friends, your business associates, your favorite television shows and movies, the news programs you watch, the talk radio hosts you respect, and even the billboard advertisements you see as you are driving down the road.

Your belief system controls what you see and therefore your perception of reality. What you believe will set your boundaries and limitations in life. Those boundaries and limitations will either be set by God's Word and His Spirit or by all of the enemy's and the world's influences.

Your belief system also attracts and repels. If you are full of faith in God and His Word, you will attract those who also are full of faith in God and His Word—and those who want to be. You will repel and often offend those who are the enemies of God and His Word. Even those unbelievers you maintain a good relationship with will always be under the conviction of the Holy Spirit in your presence, so there will be a level of tension between you until they receive Jesus and come into God's Kingdom.

Your belief system will bring success or failure into your life. If you believe God is for you, that He loves you, that He values and respects you, and that He is a Father who always has your best interest at heart, then you will walk in His love and favor. On the other hand, if you believe God is your judge and jury, always scrutinizing your every thought, word, and deed; waiting for you to sin or make a mistake; and making you sick to teach you something—chances are you will walk in fear, condemnation, and judgmentalism.

You see in yourself and the world around you what you believe God sees in you. The core of your belief system has to do with who you believe God is and how God sees you.

THERMOMETER OR THERMOSTAT?

There are two kinds of people in this world: thermometers and thermostats. A thermometer always picks up what the room temperature is and reflects that. A thermostat sets the temperature and brings the room to that setting. God wants us to be His thermostats. No matter where we go or what situation we are in, we do not let anyone but God dictate how we think, what we say, and what we do. We don't walk into a room and conform to everyone else in that room. We walk into a room and set the spiritual temperature! We bring the presence of Almighty God and the truth of His eternal Word into that room.

The interesting thing about thermostats is that they can work only when they are connected to the right power source. Our power source is our Father God. For us to set the right spiritual temperature wherever we go, then we have to be operating in the power of God. In practical, everyday terms, that means we have to have our minds renewed to His Word and be walking in His Spirit.

We have talked about how we were created to love and be loved by God. But let's go back to our creation and see just how deep this thing goes.

> God said, Let the earth bring forth grass, the herb yielding seed, and the fruit tree yielding fruit after his kind, whose seed is in itself, upon the earth: and it was so.
>
> And the earth brought forth grass, and herb yielding seed after his kind, and the tree yielding fruit, whose seed was in itself, after his kind: and God saw that it was good.
>
> Genesis 1:11-12

God called grass, herbs, and trees out of the earth. All plant life grows up out of the earth. Now what would happen if you pulled that grass out of the dirt? What would happen to your apple tree if you uprooted it from the ground?

God said, Let the waters bring forth abundantly the moving creature that hath life, and fowl that may fly above the earth in the open firmament of heaven.

And God created great whales, and every living creature that moveth, which the waters brought forth abundantly, after their kind, and every winged fowl after his kind: and God saw that it was good.

Genesis 1:20-21

God called the fish, whales, and all sea creatures out of the waters. He also created birds to fly through the air. What would happen to a catfish if you took it out of the water and threw it on the ground? What would happen to an eagle if it was placed in a small cage and couldn't even flap its wings?

When you separate the creation from its source of creation, it ceases to function correctly and begins to die.

God said, Let us make man in our image, after our likeness: and let them have dominion over the fish of the sea, and over the fowl of the air, and over the cattle, and over all the earth, and over every creeping thing that creepeth upon the earth.

Genesis 1:26

God called plants out of the soil and fish out of the sea, but He called mankind out of Himself. He is the Source of our lives! When we became separated from Him by Adam's sin, we died spiritually and ceased to function as we were created to function. Our lives became frightening, confusing, and full of grief.

When we are born again, we are restored to our Source of Life. We can now function as we were created to function, and we have the assurance and security of eternal life. Death has no more power over us. We will live forever with our Father in Heaven. We are like an uprooted tree that has been replanted into the richest soil imaginable.

The power of our spiritual connection—our salvation— is that we are no longer thermometers, conforming to every worldly belief, every charming or intelligent person, and every demonic influence that comes our way. No longer do we live the low life, following our physical senses and natural minds. Our perception of reality has been radically changed. We are born again into the Kingdom of God, where we live by faith in the Spirit and the Word of God. We have been restored to the high life in Him.

THE CHOICE IS STILL YOURS

What grieves the Holy Spirit more than anything else is to see a born-again, Spirit-filled believer continuing to live the low life. How does this happen? They are still making choices based upon their physical senses and natural thinking. Their perception is still based upon their carnal thoughts and physical senses instead of God's Word and the teaching of the Holy Spirit.

When a believer's mind is not being continually renewed with God's Word, their perception is not based on a belief system that is consistent with Scripture. Their perception is based upon what the devil, the world, and their flesh has told them. Therefore, their choices are going to tend to be unscriptural and ungodly. Their lives will not reflect the light of Jesus Christ. In fact, you might wonder if they are really saved.

Like the children of Israel who saw themselves as grasshoppers instead of more than conquerors, believers whose minds are not renewed will see themselves as sinners saved by grace, barely getting by, instead of winners in Christ Jesus. The children of Israel chose the low life because they were judging their situation according to their physical senses and carnal thinking. If they had seen their situation through the eyes of God and His Word, like Joshua and Caleb, they would have chosen the high life. They would have entered the Promised Land, defeated the giants, shouted till every wall fell down flat, and then enjoyed the luxuries and benefits God had provided for them.

It doesn't matter what you are going through in life, you will always be given two reports. One will be evil. It will be based upon human perception and reasoning. The other will be good, and it will be based upon Heaven's perception, which is given in the Word and by the Spirit of God. You will choose to believe the evil report or the good report, and the quality and impact of your life will be determined by which report you choose to believe.

PICTURE PERFECT

We operate and live by pictures in our minds. If I tell you about my dog, you don't think d-o-g. You have a picture in your mind of a dog. The more details and the better I describe my dog, the clearer the picture on the inside of you. From that moment on, whenever I speak about my dog, you will automatically "see" my dog in your mind.

God designed us to be visual. We have physical eyes and spiritual eyes. Our physical eyes see what is going on in the physical world; our spiritual eyes see what is going on in the spiritual realm. But remember, we really see with our minds. That's why God tells us to meditate in His Word day and night. Then our spiritual eyes can judge the spirit realm rightly. His Word is truth, and His truth will enable us to discern whether or not what we are seeing is from God or the devil.

Also, remember that the devil blinds the minds of the unbelieving. He does not put blinders over their physical or spiritual eyes. He comes to steal the Word out of their minds and hearts so that they will be blind to his schemes and destruction. Then he can lead people where he wants them to go and get them to do what he wants them to do. They will think they are doing the right thing, but they are really causing trouble in their lives and the lives of everyone they touch. All because their perception—what their minds believe and the pictures they see—are based on the devil's lies.

The children of Israel were filled with unbelief, and the only way they could be filled with unbelief was if they chose not to meditate and believe what God said to them. They could only picture themselves being trampled by the giants, and dying in the wilderness. But Joshua and Caleb had a different picture in their minds. They saw themselves as more than conquerors, because that is the picture God's promise put in them when they chose to believe it. They took the Promised Land and lived successful, fulfilled lives in it—just like they had pictured.

What kind of picture do you have of you? Is it the picture the Bible paints or the picture the world paints? Your perception of who you are determines who you become, so you can't just sit and think about anything that comes into your mind. You must discipline your thought life by meditating in God's Word. Then you will have a godly perception of everyone and everything.

THE POWER OF PICTURES

One day I was flipping through the channels on the television and came across something that astonished me. There was a vampire walking into a church, and he marched right up to the cross, tore it off the wall, walked out of the church with it, and then proceeded to hide it. I sat there with my mouth hanging open because that was not what the movies had taught me was true! Remember, I grew up watching horror movies, and no vampire ever went near a cross! Anyone with any sense knew that a cross would stop a vampire in his tracks and debilitate him.

I turned off the television and began to think about this in light of the Word of God. Since the devil is blinding the minds of the unbelieving, he is always lying. Now he was trying to plant a picture in the hearts of people that the Cross of Jesus Christ had no power or authority over vampires or any evil being in this world. That was a picture I chose to reject and eject from my mind and heart. I took that thought, that picture, captive and threw it out! Then I began meditating on what was true and real.

> Now I know that the Lord is greater than all gods: for in the thing wherein they dealt proudly he was above them.
>
> Exodus 18:11

My mind was filled with pictures of God defeating one Egyptian god after another through Moses. If God defeated all those gods that had such a tight hold on the Egyptian people, a vampire was no problem for Him! There was nothing that could stand before Him!

> Ye are of God, little children, and have overcome them: because greater is he that is in you, than he that is in the world.
>
> 1 John 4:4

Because I am His child and I am of God, anything He overcomes I can overcome too. There is nothing and nobody in this world greater than my God, and He is in me and I am in Him!

There is only one reason I did not go to bed that night scared out of my wits of vampires, and that is because I chose to meditate and believe God's Word. I pondered and muttered about the tremendous majesty and sovereignty and supernatural power of my Father God. Then I rejoiced that I was in Him and He was in me. With that perfect picture of the truth established in my mind and heart, it was impossible for me to perceive a vampire as any kind of a threat to me or anyone else.

You may say, "Well, vampires are not real! Couldn't you just know that and forget the whole thing?"

My Bible says to guard my mind and heart, and I take that very seriously because what I perceive in my heart, what I believe to be true, all the pictures I carry inside of me—that is what I will become. Whether it is real or not, we must rid our minds of any image from the enemy. We must give him no place in our thoughts.

Real or not, your perception of reality is what your life will become.

THE DIFFERENCE BETWEEN ABRAM AND LOT

And Abram was very rich in cattle, in silver, and in gold....

And Lot also, which went with Abram, had flocks, and herds, and tents.

And the land was not able to bear them, that they might dwell together: for their substance was great, so that they could not dwell together.

> And there was a strife between the herdmen of Abram's cattle and the herdmen of Lot's cattle.
>
> Genesis 13:2,5-7

Lot followed his Uncle Abram until they both were so wealthy that it became impossible for them to live together any longer. Lot's herdsmen were fighting with Abram's herdsmen, and it was time for the two to separate into two households. Abram gave Lot first choice of land, and Lot made an interesting decision.

> Lot chose him all the plain of Jordan; and Lot journeyed east: and they separated themselves the one from the other.
>
> Abram dwelled in the land of Canaan, and Lot dwelled in the cities of the plain, and pitched his tent toward Sodom.
>
> But the men of Sodom were wicked and sinners before the Lord exceedingly.
>
> Genesis 13:11-13

Lot chose to live near Sodom, which was not a very nice place. Every day Lot woke up and his eyes saw more and more pictures of evil, implanting wickedness in his mind and heart. His family and servants were also subject to this repeatedly.

Because we always move in the direction of the images we have inside us, Lot began to move his family closer and closer to Sodom. Eventually they moved right into the city and lived among all those people whose hearts were turned against God. Everyone they knew there was pursuing sin and wickedness, so you can guess what their perception of life became and how they began to live their lives.

Ask anyone who has become hooked on pornography, and they will tell you it all began quite innocently. They were just looking at a few pictures. Lot was the same way. He just wanted his family to live in a fruitful land, but he repeatedly looked more toward Sodom as his source than he looked to God as his Source. Sodom provided him with a number of pictures that captured his heart and mind, pulling him and his family away from God and everything that was good in life. The enemy also knows we operate by pictures!

If you are still questioning the power that what we see repeatedly becomes our standard and value, there was one football player who was paid to wear a Nike product while he was out in public. Every time he wore their product, Nike's sales went up one hundred thousand dollars. That is the power of an image in the minds of people! We gravitate toward what we picture and meditate on in our minds.

What was the difference between Abram and Lot? The pictures in their minds. Lot's mind was filled with evil words and actions. Abram had a different picture, a picture God designed. In Genesis 15 He told Abram to look at the stars of the sky because that was a picture of his descendants. Abram began to see himself as a father of nations, and particularly of a great nation that would carry God's Word and bring forth the Messiah.

It is clear that what made the difference in these two men's lives was their perception of who God was and who they were in relation to God. Lot didn't honor God or take His Word seriously. His perception of life was based on his carnal thinking and physical pleasure, and his life and his family ended in ruins.

Abram honored God more than anything or anyone else, and he believed and obeyed the word of the Lord. Abram's perception of life was based on God's Word and will, and his life and his family flourished.

> He staggered not at the promise of God through unbelief; but was strong in faith, giving glory to God;
> And being fully persuaded that, what he had promised, he was able also to perform.
> And therefore it was imputed to him for righteousness.
>
> Romans 4:20-22

While Lot got up every morning and looked toward Sodom, Abram had been counting stars every night! He had such a clear picture of God's faithfulness, that when God told him to sacrifice his only son Isaac, he did it without batting an eyelash! He marched up that mountain and told everyone that both of them would be coming back!

> By faith Abraham, when he was tried, offered up Isaac: and he that had received the promises offered up his only begotten son,
> Of whom it was said, That in Isaac shall thy seed be called:

Accounting that God was able to raise him up, even from the dead; from whence also he received him in a figure.

Hebrews 11:17-19

Abram didn't know *how* God was going to keep His promise, but he knew He *would* keep it. Why was he so sure? Because he believed and had a picture of God's promise deep on the inside of him. God's Word was reality. He knew God had created him to be Abraham, a father of nations.

The vision God gave Abram and the belief system that God is greater than any natural circumstance or obstacle formed Abram's perception. And we know that his perception is what he became. He became Abraham, a thermostat for God, who changed the spiritual climate in which he lived and made a tremendous impact on human history.

CHAPTER 17

EXTRAVAGANT LOVE

We have known and believed the love that God hath to us.
God is love; and he that dwelleth in love dwelleth in God,
and God in him.

1 John 4:16

The Bible says that God is love. He embodies love.
Everything He does is motivated by love and is an expression of His love. The Good News is that His love has an
object, and that object is you! And He isn't just loving with
no purpose. He loves with the purpose of seeing you
become all He created you to be. He wants you to succeed
and to be happy.

Jesus said that when we look at Him, we are looking at
the Father (see John 14:9). Therefore, Jesus also is love. He
is the manifested love of God in this Earth, and He revealed
and sealed that love by dying on the Cross for our sins and
then being resurrected from the dead to give us the new

birth. This was the greatest act of love this universe will ever see, and He did it for you!

God went to all this trouble so that you could become His child and live with Him forever, but along with that came all the benefits in this life of being a joint-heir with Jesus Christ. His love for you desires to see you live like a king under the King of kings from the moment you are born again. He desires for you to be more than a conqueror because He wants to love others through you. He wants to work in you and through you to reach your family, your co-workers, your neighbors, your city, your nation, and the world. As His child you are to express and reflect His love to everyone you meet.

Once you were born again, you took on superman or superwoman status in the area of love. You now have the fruit of the Holy Spirit operating in you, and the first fruit and main fruit, which is the foundation for all the other fruit, is love. You are now able to choose to walk in God's love, which means you have the supernatural disposition of God. You can love folks who don't want to be loved. You can love people who give you no reason to love them. You can even love those who are just downright mean and wicked!

As a child of God and joint-heir with Jesus, you have the capacity to love those who don't love you back. You can love those who hate you, persecute you, mock you, make fun of you, and lie about you. But there's more. You have the capacity to love those who hurt the people who are most precious to you. You can love your enemies and your loved ones' enemies. You can pray for them, declare God's Word over them, and have faith that they will be saved, healed, and set free from all their wicked ways.

HOW THE RIDICULOUS BECOMES LOGICAL

At this point you are probably saying, "How is that possible? I might be able to forgive someone who hurt my spouse or my child, but don't tell me I have to love them! That's just the most ridiculous thing I ever heard."

No, the most ridiculous thing you ever heard was God becoming a man and dying for you when all you did was use His name to cuss people out, when you were a liar and a manipulator, when all you could think about was yourself and getting what you wanted, and when you went around hurting others to achieve your own pleasure. Who would die for that kind of person? Jesus did when He died for you. Now wasn't that ridiculous?

When you think about it, very little that God does makes sense or seems logical to our natural minds. Was it very logical to march around the walls of Jericho for seven days and then blow the trumpets? That would probably not have been your battle plan. And then He chose a shepherd boy to defeat a giant, and the boy did it with just a sling and a stone. Finally, Jesus came as a human being and proceeded not only to forgive tax collectors and prostitutes, but also He welcomed them into His ministry! What would you think if your pastor did stuff like that?

Obviously, there is a gap between how natural human beings think and how God thinks. His concept of love and our natural concept of love are completely different. Now we know that He didn't save us to come down to our level of thinking. He saved us to bring us up to His level of thinking. He wants to conform us to the image of Jesus so that we will love like He loves. Loving like God is the key to everything in the Christian life.

Loving like God and thinking like God are the same thing.

LOVING MEANS KNOWING

We are of God: he that knoweth God heareth us; he that is not of God heareth not us. Hereby know we the spirit of truth, and the spirit of error.

Beloved, let us love one another: for love is of God; and every one that loveth is born of God, and knoweth God.

He that loveth not knoweth not God; for God is love.

1 John 4:6-8

When we are born again, we know the love of God for the first time. It is not a feeling or an emotion, although we can have a very strong emotional response to His love. We experience His love in our spirits, where the reality of being His child, His chosen, and His beloved is made known by His Holy Spirit. We get a revelation of our new life in Him.

To continue growing in this revelation and to be transformed into the image of Jesus Christ, we must continue to receive God's love and truth, and we do that by abiding in

His Word. By meditating in His Word day and night, we get to know Him better and better every day. Slowly but surely, we begin to think, speak, and act more like Him. This is how we begin to see the logic and the real sense in everything He does.

As our minds are changed by God's Word, we begin to live and make decisions from our spirits, according to the Word and the Spirit, instead of our natural thinking and physical senses. Marching seven times around formidable walls, silently meditating on the promise of God and having faith in His promise, suddenly seems exactly the right thing to do. Having a young man kill a giant with a sling and a rock makes perfect sense to us. Why? Because we love God and know God.

We are capable not only of forgiving but loving and praying for those who use and abuse us. The compassion of God inside us readily understands that those who do evil and hurt others do not know the love of God as we do. Like Jesus on the Cross, we can say, "Father, forgive them. They don't know what they are doing" (see Luke 23:34). This doesn't mean we do not hold people accountable for their actions, but we can continue in God's love for them while we do the right thing.

> We henceforth [will] be no more children, tossed to and fro, and carried about with every wind of doctrine, by the sleight of men, and cunning craftiness, whereby they lie in wait to deceive;

But speaking the truth in love, may grow up into him in all things, which is the head, even Christ:

From whom the whole body fitly joined together and compacted by that which every joint supplieth, according to the effectual working in the measure of every part, maketh increase of the body unto the edifying of itself in love.

Ephesians 4:14-16

The body of Christ will succeed only in fulfilling God's will by loving and knowing God. That is how we will love one another and get properly connected, and Jesus said in John 13:34-35 that the only way the world is going to recognize we are His disciples is when they see how we love each other. When the world takes notice at how we take care of our poor, our needy, our uneducated, and those among us who are caught in sin and bondage—they are going to see Jesus! They are going to want to be a part of that kind of love.

DON'T WALK AS GENTILES

This I say therefore, and testify in the Lord, that ye henceforth walk not as other Gentiles walk, in the vanity of their mind,

Having the understanding darkened, being alienated from the life of God through the ignorance that is in them, because of the blindness of their heart:

Who being past feeling have given themselves over unto lasciviousness, to work all uncleanness with greediness.

But ye have not so learned Christ.

Ephesians 4:17-20

If the Bible tells us not to walk like the Gentiles, in the vanity of our minds, that must mean that it is possible for us to be born again and walk in darkness. God would not tell us not to do something unless we were capable of doing it. He also says that walking in the vanity of our carnal thinking is not how we learn Christ. We learn Christ by abiding in His Word.

> Grace and peace be multiplied unto you through the knowledge of God, and of Jesus our Lord,
>
> According as his divine power hath given unto us all things that pertain unto life and godliness, through the knowledge of him that hath called us to glory and virtue:
>
> Whereby are given unto us exceeding great and precious promises: that by these ye might be partakers of the divine nature, having escaped the corruption that is in the world through lust.
>
> 2 Peter 1:2-4

We literally partake of the divine nature of God and Jesus Christ by simply believing and living by the promises of God in His Word. Grace and peace are multiplied through the knowledge of God and Christ. The more we know Him, the more we love Him, and the more we can receive all He wants to give us.

Let me tell you why the body of Christ is not walking in all things pertaining unto life and godliness. A believer—let's call him Ray—will hear the Word of God at church, get all excited about what he heard, and then go home and tell his friends Bubba and Lucretia about it. Bubba and Lucretia aren't saved, or maybe they are saved and not serving God right now. All of a sudden they come against Ray. They argue that nothing he's telling them makes sense. They tell him he's being brainwashed. They tell him that the pastor just wants his money. They remind Ray of all the hypocrisy and sin in the church today. They ask, "How can you trust any of them?"

These people are thinking like Gentiles. Their understanding is dark. They have no light because they are not abiding in the truth of God's Word or following His Spirit. Yet Ray will listen to them and consider what they say because he loves them and cares what they think. The question is, does he love them and care what they think more than he loves God and what He thinks?

Ray listens, and instead of taking everything Bubba and Lucretia say about God and asking Him for wisdom, he begins to think for himself. He doesn't open his Bible. He doesn't pray in the Spirit and meditate in the Word. Before you know it, he begins backing off his prayer time. He still goes to church, but more and more he has a skeptical, critical attitude. Soon he stops giving, and eventually he stops going to church altogether.

Our friend Ray listened to people who walked like the Gentiles instead of sticking to the Word and the Spirit. He forgot that he was not born again by his work or anyone else's work. He was born again through the work of the Holy Spirit and the Word of God, and that is how he is supposed to live. Jesus is his life. He is the way and the truth and the life (see John 14:6).

Bubba and Lucretia don't know or love God, and they will never see Him if Ray doesn't begin to renew his mind and get back into fellowship with God and other believers.

Ray will sink into living the low life if he listens to his friends. And what's worse, his friends will never see Jesus in Ray until he is transformed by God's Word and loves the saints regardless of their faults and failures. Again, love is the key here. We must love God and know God to succeed in life, and we cannot know Him or love Him apart from His Word.

LIVING THE HIGH LIFE

The key to living the high life is found in a passage of Scripture we have repeated throughout this book.

I beseech you therefore, brethren, by the mercies of God, that ye present your bodies a living sacrifice, holy, acceptable unto God, which is your reasonable service.

And be not conformed to this world, but be ye transformed by the renewing of your mind, that ye may prove what is that good, and acceptable, and perfect, will of God.

Romans 12:1-2

The benefits and rewards of being transformed by the renewing of our minds are beyond our ability to imagine because our minds cannot grasp the full measure of God's love for us or His desire to bless us. However, Jesus showed us again and again just how extravagant God's love for us was.

> He [Jesus] entered into one of the ships, which was Simon's, and prayed him that he would thrust out a little from the land. And he sat down, and taught the people out of the ship.
>
> Now when he had left speaking, he said unto Simon, Launch out into the deep, and let down your nets for a draught.
>
> Luke 5:3-4

What do you think Jesus was teaching the people? He was preaching the Gospel, telling them that God loved them and wanted a relationship with them. He was giving them the Good News that God wanted to bless them. All they had to do was give Him their whole heart and have faith in Him to protect them and provide for them in every situation, just like He promised in His Word.

After teaching the people about the power of salvation, Jesus wanted to demonstrate it. He asked Simon Peter to launch his boat and go fishing.

> Simon answering said unto him, Master, we have toiled all the night, and have taken nothing: nevertheless at thy word I will let down the net.
>
> And when they had this done, they inclosed a great multitude of fishes: and their net brake.
>
> And they beckoned unto their partners, which were in the other ship, that they should come and help them. And they came, and filled both the ships, so that they began to sink.
>
> Luke 5:5-7

Now this is where most saints miss the high life because they don't think like God. They say things like, "Why did God give them all that fish? They didn't need so much. They could have had a fine feast with just enough for all of them and a little more to sell when they needed to repair the boat and buy a new net. And what about the other fishermen on that lake? Were there any fish left for them? Think how long it will take to repopulate that lake!"

These are the same saints who accuse believers of being greedy when they believe God for big profits, financial wealth, and superabundance in money and material goods. They are so locked into natural thinking and false humility that they believe there are only so many fish to go around and no one should have that kind of superabundance. They don't have any knowledge of how big God is, and they have completely missed His extravagant love for them.

I will tell you the truth. A saint whose mind has been renewed to know God's extravagant love for them will not love and worship what God has given them. They have only one reaction when God blesses them.

> When Simon Peter saw it, he fell down at Jesus' knees, saying, Depart from me; for I am a sinful man, O Lord.
> For he was astonished, and all that were with him, at the draught of the fishes which they had taken:
>
> Luke 5:8-9

Every fisherman and every person who witnessed the incredible—even ridiculous—catch of fish that came as a result of simply obeying the word of the Lord was aston-ished. They were astonished because they had never believed God loved them so much. Peter immediately hit his knees, repented, and called Jesus his Lord. He saw the extravagant love of Jesus and felt the weight of his own sin and selfishness.

Peter's reaction to this amazing, supernatural catch of fish is a clear demonstration of the fact that it is the good-ness of God that leads people to repent (see Romans 2:4). He cried that he was a sinful man and repented of his narrow, evil perception of God. He repented of all the boundaries and limitations he had placed upon the love God had for him. He repented because he now knew that the God of the Universe desired for him to prosper in every area of his life.

The most generous, loving, giving people on the face of the Earth today are believers who fully accept and walk in the extravagant love of God. They are not groveling and begging for every dollar and morsel of food. They are walking in faith, knowing their loving Heavenly Father has already provided everything they need in Christ Jesus. They are not feeling sorry for themselves because someone offended them, because the love of God in them can only forgive. And that love can't help spilling out of them to everyone around them.

Living the high life is being able to love extravagantly the way God loves.

CONCLUSION

The high life in Jesus Christ encompasses a lot of important issues in our lives, and the most important is that we are one with the Father, the Son, and the Holy Spirit. Our *koinonia* with the Godhead is the foundation for everything else we enjoy in the high life. But that "everything else" comes only by renewing our minds with the Word of God.

What God has deposited into our spirits must be released into our souls and our bodies: His love, joy, peace, wisdom, holy character, and courage will flow through us and transform us only when we meditate and abide in His Word. Then "everything else" in our lives manifests.

We have the grace and wisdom to repulse sin and live holy, consecrated lives unto God.

We have no fear of the devil or any demonic spirit.

We can forgive and move forward after being offended and hurt; and when we hurt and offend someone else we can repent and ask for forgiveness.

We have great marriages and raise up children for the Lord.

We have wonderful friends, saints who will encourage us, pray for us, and help us stay straight in a crooked world.

We are successful in our professions and ministries, and while we enjoy what we do, we make an impact for Jesus.

We believe and receive everything we need materially and financially, and that means more than enough to provide for our families and to help others in need.

We walk in divine health and healing, knowing the purpose of our physical bodies is to be God's house and serve Him and His people.

Our whole life is about Jesus, not ourselves.

And we have eternal vision. We are not tied to the physical realm. We are not led by our natural thinking. That was the low life we lived before Jesus. Now we live according to the living, active, powerful Word of God. We walk according to the Spirit and not the flesh. We move in the magnificent grace of God, enjoying His extravagant love—living the high life!

ENDNOTES

Chapter 1—Who's Got Your Soul?

[1] James Strong, *Exhaustive Concordance of the Bible*, "Greek Dictionary of the New Testament," (Nashville, TN: Thomas Nelson Publishers, 1984), #3339.

[2] *Webster's New World College Dictionary*, Third Edition, Victoria Neufeldt, Editor-in-Chief (New York: Macmillan, Inc., 1996), p. 852.

Chapter 4—Leaving Your Comfort Zone

[1] James Strong, *Exhaustive Concordance of the Bible*, "Greek Dictionary of the New Testament," #2072.

Chapter 5—Learning to Think Right

[1] http://en.wikipedia.org/wiki/Me_and_Mrs._Jones

Chapter 6—Don't Fence Me In!

[1] James Strong, *Exhaustive Concordance of the Bible*, "Hebrew and Chaldee Dictionary," #8444.

Chapter 7—*Koinonia*

[1] Spiros Zodhiates, *The Complete Word Study Dictionary:* New Testament, (Chattanooga, TN: AMG Publishers, 1992), p. 873.

[2] Ibid., p. 766.

Chapter 8—The Law of Meditation

[1] James Strong, *Exhaustive Concordance of the Bible*, "Hebrew and Chaldee Dictionary," #7878.

[2] Ibid., #1897.

[3] Ibid., #7878.

Chapter 10—How Long Are You Slack?

[1] Spiros Zodhiates, *Hebrew-Greek Key Word Study Bible* "Lexical Aids to the Old Testament" (Chattanooga, TN: AMG Publishers, 1984, 1991), p. 1661.

[2] James Strong, *Exhaustive Concordance of the Bible,* "Hebrew and Chaldee Dictionary," #8444.

Chapter 15—The Lessons of Jericho

[1] James Strong, *Exhaustive Concordance of the Bible,* "Hebrew and Chaldee Dictionary," #6754.

[2] Ibid., #1823.

PRAYER OF SALVATION

God loves you—no matter who you are, no matter what your past. God loves you so much that He gave His one and only begotten Son for you. The Bible tells us that "...whoever believes in him shall not perish but have eternal life" (John 3:16 NIV). Jesus laid down His life and rose again so that we could spend eternity with Him in Heaven and experience His absolute best on earth. If you would like to receive Jesus into your life, say the following prayer out loud and mean it from your heart:

Heavenly Father, I come to You admitting that I am a sinner. Right now, I choose to turn away from sin, and I ask You to cleanse me of all unrighteousness. I believe that Your Son, Jesus, died on the cross to take away my sins. I also believe that He rose again from the dead so that I might be forgiven of my sins and made righteous through faith in Him. I call upon the name of Jesus Christ to be the Savior and Lord of my life. Jesus, I choose to follow You and ask that You fill me with the power of the Holy Spirit. I declare that right now I am a child of God. I am free from sin and full of the righteousness of God. I am saved in Jesus' name. Amen.

If you prayed this prayer to receive Jesus Christ as your Savior for the first time, please contact us on the Web at **www.bwm.org** to receive a free book.

Or you may write to us at
Bill Winston Ministries
P.O. Box 947
Oak Park, IL 60303

ABOUT THE AUTHOR

Bill Winston is a visionary leader whose mission is to empower believers through teaching and preaching the uncompromised Word of God, and to fulfill their highest calling and change the world through Jesus Christ.

Bill Winston received his Honorary Doctorate of Humane Letters from Friends International Christian University, and is Founder and Pastor of Living Word Christian Center, an 18,000-member church located in Forest Park, Illinois, and Tuskegee Christian Center in Tuskegee, Alabama. The church has a broad range of entities including: the Joseph Business School (which includes a campus and on-line business school); Living Word School of Ministry and Missions; the Forest Park Plaza (a 32-acre shopping mall) and Washington Plaza (a shopping center in Tuskegee); Living Word Christian Academy; and many others. He also hosts the *Believer's Walk of Faith* television and radio broadcast, which reaches more than 200 million households nationwide and overseas.

Pastor Winston is also the Founder and Chairman of The Joseph Center® for Business Development, Chairman of the Board of Covenant Bank, President of New Covenant Community Development Corporation, Founder of Bill Winston Ministries (a ministry outreach that shares the Gospel through television, radio, and other media), and President and Founder of Faith Ministries Alliance (FMA), an alliance of more than 350 churches and ministries under the covering of Pastor Winston in the U.S. and overseas.

Pastor Winston is married to Veronica and is the father of three children, Melody, Nicole, and David.

To contact Bill Winston Ministries,
please write or call
P.O. Box 947
Oak Park, IL 60303
708-697-5100
or visit him on the Web at
www.bwm.org

Please include your prayer requests
and comments when you write.

THE KINGDOM OF GOD IN YOU

If the Kingdom of God is in us, why aren't we living lives of greatness in our world?

There are two kingdoms at work in this world, and tragically, even within the church, the majority of people are still living under the destructive lies and patterns of Satan's rule.

Bill Winston helps believers to start walking out their faith in miraculous ways. Why? We have a power within us that is supernatural and flies in the face of the world's arrogant—but ultimately inadequate—self-reliance on human understanding and effort.

With the faith of a child, even as small as a mustard seed, we unleash God's provision and power in our lives not by focusing on what we want, but by asking what the King of the Kingdom, God Almighty, wants us to accomplish. We quickly discover that our "grand dreams" and aspirations are miniscule in light of the greatness He has in store for us to do.

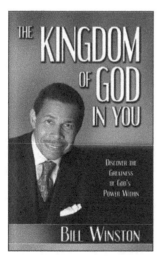

The Kingdom of God in You
Bill Winston
978-1-57794-796-7

The Kingdom of God in You
Unabridged Audio Book
5 CDs
978-1-57794-997-8

The Kingdom of God in You Digital
Download for iTunes
978-1-57794-990-9

Available at bookstores everywhere
or visit **www.harrisonhouse.com.**

THE LAW OF CONFESSION

Just like natural laws, there are spiritual laws with cause and effect. God set the universe in motion with the power of His words and established the law of confession, but many believers have suffered needlessly by misunderstanding the power of their words.

Dr. Bill Winston reveals scriptural examples and vital teaching on the importance of the spoken word. Uncover the enemy's deceptive plan to use your own words against you and what you can do to turn your situation around.

Controlling your words is one of the biggest challenges anyone will face in this life; the Bible reveals the power of life and death are in the words you say. As you begin to change the words you speak, you will rewrite your future and revolutionize your life.

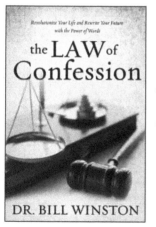

The Law of Confession

978-1-57794-969-5

Available at bookstores everywhere
or visit **www.harrisonhouse.com.**

Fast. Easy.
Convenient.

For the latest Harrison House product information and author news, look no further than your computer. All the details on our powerful, life-changing products are just a click away. New releases, E-mail subscriptions, Podcasts, testimonies, monthly specials—find it all in one place. Visit harrisonhouse.com today!

harrisonhouse

THE HARRISON HOUSE VISION

Proclaiming the truth and the power

Of the Gospel of Jesus Christ

With excellence;

Challenging Christians to

Live victoriously,

Grow spiritually,

Know God intimately.